I0018005

<prompt>
DOT AI
2025 Edition

Art of Writing Generative AI Prompts

Da Sachin Sharma

Copyright © 2025 da sachin sharma

All Rights Reserved.

This book has been self-published with all reasonable efforts taken to make the material error-free by the author. No part of this book shall be used, reproduced in any manner whatsoever without written permission from the author, except in the case of brief quotations embodied in critical articles and reviews.

The Author of this book is solely responsible and liable for its content including but not limited to the views, representations, descriptions, statements, information, opinions and references ["Content"]. The Content of this book shall not constitute or be construed or be deemed to reflect the opinion or expression of the Publisher or Editor. Neither the Publisher nor Editor endorse or approve the Content of this book or guarantee the reliability, accuracy or completeness of the Content published herein and do not make any representations or warranties of any kind, express or implied, including but not limited to the implied warranties of merchantability, fitness for a particular purpose. The Publisher and Editor shall not be liable whatsoever for any errors, omissions, whether such errors or omissions result from negligence, accident, or any other cause or claims for loss or damages of any kind, including without limitation, indirect or consequential loss or damage arising out of use, inability to use, or about the reliability, accuracy or sufficiency of the information contained in this book.

Dedication

The year that passed between the 2024 and 2025 editions of this book was one of breathtaking change— not just in the landscape of artificial intelligence, but in the landscape of my own life. While the world was busy adapting to new models and algorithms, my world was learning to navigate a new reality without two of its most important people.

This book is, therefore, dedicated to their loving memory.

*To my father, **Poonam Chand Sharma**. Your guidance was my compass, and your belief in me was my foundation. The world feels quieter without you. I miss you, Papa.*

*And to my dear friend, **Ashish Sharma**. Always the first to buy my books, always the first to cheer me on. Your friendship was a gift, and your absence is deeply felt. Gone too soon.*

This work is a testament to their memory, a reminder that even in a world of constant, overwhelming change, it is the love we share and the people we lose that give our creations true meaning and purpose.

I miss you...

*This book is dedicated to my beloved wife, Vidhi Angria,
my daughter, the talented writer Da Sashyavi Sharma,
and my mother Varsha Sharma, thank you for helping
shape me into the person I am today*

Contents

9

Foreword

As a creativity and innovation coach, I am asked every day, will human creativity survive? Will creative artists be able to sustain in this AI world?

The quick answer is an emphatic YES. But we must be prepared for new ways of doing things.

We are on the cusp, between the old world and the new world. The AI is here, almost here, to demolish the myth that only creative people can make words sing and only they have the power to embed emotions in colors and pixels.

AI's shockwaves are felt across the creative world – from writers to art directors to painters and artisans – everyone is asking, what next?

And no one knows. Because the technology is developing so fast, by the time you learn the new trick, it is old.

Now imagine an overwhelmed creative person putting a prompt to the universe:

Give me a master key to open the secrets of AI tools and techniques. A master code that will work in spite of all the new developments. A mantra which helps me be on top of the AI game, not just today but tomorrow and the day after. I need a solution that can help me ride this AI wave with confidence.

Or imagine a business executive getting frustrated and asking:

I have the latest versions of AI tools but even then why can't I get the results like I see on social media?

And then, both of them would receive the book that's in your hand. Or on your screen.

I feel Prompt DOT AI is not just another book on AI.

This book by Da Sachin demonstrates the human caring in the AI world. As I went through the book, I could sense his presence on every single page. As an AI trainer, he knows all the pitfalls that users make. And he helps you steer through them so well.

This is not another book about various tools and platforms. It is not another compilation of prompts. Rather, it helps us, the readers, how to create our own prompts.

It helps us develop our own approach towards using AI. Which means, whatever may be the new tool in town, you would be able to get the best results.

As a creativity coach, my suggestion is: Use the book as a primer for developing your AI competency. You will reap the rewards for a long time.

This book gives you wings. Where you wish to fly is up to you!

I wish you great ideas!

Puneet Bhatnagar
Creativity & Success Coach
www.creacos.com

Preface to the 2025 Edition

As we step into the latter half of 2025, the landscape of artificial intelligence has undergone another year of breathtaking evolution. The rapid transformation that characterized 2024 has not slowed; it has accelerated, specialized, and matured, reshaping the contours of human creativity and professional work in ways that demand a new level of understanding and a new set of skills. The synergy between human ingenuity and AI capabilities has moved beyond a "new renaissance" of artistic expression into a more complex, integrated, and powerful ecosystem.

It is in this context of profound change that this updated edition of "Prompt DOT AI: Art of Writing Generative AI Prompts" is presented. The core mission of this book remains the same: to empower you to harness the full potential of AI as a collaborative partner. However, the nature of that partnership has fundamentally shifted.

The past year has been defined by three pivotal themes. First is the evolution **from general tools to**

specialized agents. In 2024, our focus was on mastering powerful, all-in-one models like ChatGPT. The landscape of 2025 is far more nuanced. We now have access to entire families of models, each fine-tuned for a specific purpose—some for logic and reasoning, others for creative writing, and still others for complex coding tasks. Consequently, the essential skill is no longer just about crafting the perfect prompt for a single AI; it is about becoming an

AI Orchestrator, strategically designing workflows that call upon a suite of specialized agents to accomplish complex goals.

Second is the **maturation of motion and the dawn of form**. AI video generation has graduated from a fascinating novelty to a viable tool for production, with platforms like Runway, Kling, and Google's Veo 3 offering sophisticated controls, high-quality output, and even synchronized audio. Simultaneously, AI-powered 3D generation has emerged as the new frontier, allowing creators to sculpt digital objects and environments with words and images, a development that was merely on the horizon a year ago.

Third is the trend of **hyper-personalization and deep integration**. AI is no longer a separate destination we visit; it is being woven into the fabric of our most-used applications and daily routines. From AI-powered features in messaging apps to the deep integration of AI into search engines and workplace software, the technology is becoming an ever-present, personalized assistant. This is reflected in the data: AI usage in the workplace has nearly doubled in the last two years, a clear sign of its move from the periphery to the core of our professional lives.

As these powerful capabilities have become more accessible, a fourth, crucial theme has come to the forefront: the **Human-in-the-Loop (HITL) imperative**. As AI systems take on more complex and critical tasks, the need for human oversight, ethical guidance, and critical thinking has moved from a philosophical debate to a practical necessity. The HITL model is now a central concept in deploying AI responsibly, ensuring that these powerful tools remain aligned with human values and real-world needs.

This 2025 edition has been thoroughly revised to reflect this new reality. Chapters on language models have been completely overhauled to guide you through the new ecosystem of specialized AIs. We introduce an entirely new chapter on the burgeoning field of AI 3D generation. Sections on video and music creation have been heavily expanded to cover the latest tools and techniques that have emerged over the past year. Throughout the book, the focus has shifted from crafting individual prompts to architecting intelligent workflows.

What has been removed? Outdated tools and techniques have been pruned to make way for the most current and effective methods. The content has been streamlined to focus on the strategic thinking required to navigate the 2025 AI landscape, ensuring you are equipped with not just the "how" but the "why" and "when" of using these incredible tools.

This book is designed for the AI Orchestrator, the creative professional who understands that the future is not about human versus AI, but about the sophisticated collaboration between human vision and a diverse team of specialized artificial intelligences. The goal is to provide you with the master key to conduct this new digital orchestra.

As we continue to write the next chapter of human-AI collaboration, my hope is that this updated edition will serve as your comprehensive guide. May it inspire you to push the boundaries of what is possible and to create works that resonate deeply in this new, exciting, and complex era.

Happy creating!

Da Sachin Sharma

Acknowledgements

In the process of creating this book, I have had the great fortune to be surrounded by a community of brilliant minds, loving hearts, and steady hands. Their collective wisdom, encouragement, and labour have made this work what it is, and it is a pleasure to acknowledge their contributions.

To begin with, my parents, whose enduring words "ja beta jeele apni zindagi" have provided me with a compass that always directs me towards living a fulfilling and meaningful life. Their unwavering faith and support in my endeavors has been a source of strength throughout this journey.

To Abhishek Porwal and Vishal Gupta, my business partners, friends, and chosen family. Thank you for standing by my side, for embracing my quirks, and for always encouraging me to follow my passions. Your trust and camaraderie mean more than words can express.

Dr. Jignesh Shah and Hetal Shah, Co-founders of Mobilla, who have not only offered me the chance to contribute to an exceptional brand but have also motivated me to infuse my knowledge and insights into our marketing strategies. I am grateful for your unwavering support.

My gratitude extends to Puneet Bhatnagar, whose words of encouragement have often been the extra nudge I needed to follow my passion, to research, to create, and to share my findings on the world stage.

I must also express my deep gratitude to the LinkedIn community, who have been generous with their feedback and engagement with my work and research. Your questions and comments have inspired me to explore further, to dig deeper, and have ultimately enriched this work.

A heartfelt thank you to my team and to the numerous individuals who have attended my workshops over time. Your curiosity, your insightful questions, and your dedication to learning have propelled me forward and fueled my motivation to continue researching and growing.

My gratitude would be incomplete without acknowledging my wife, Vidhi Angira. Her unwavering belief in my abilities, her patience, and her support have been my guiding light through the challenges and victories alike. Her encouragement is my daily motivation and the bedrock of my creative pursuits.

Last but not least, I would like to acknowledge my editor Harshita, who was there for me at the last minute and provided me with the support I needed to publish this book. Thank you, Harshita, for your tireless efforts and for being such an important part of this project.

I am indebted to each and every one of you for contributing to this journey in your unique ways. Together, we are charting a course towards a future where AI and creativity coexist and co-create. I am privileged to be part of this community and to share this journey with you. I hope that this book inspires and empowers you to navigate and thrive in the world of AI.

In the future,
it's not human versus AI, but a collaboration that
combines the best of both worlds.
-da sachin sharma

Introduction to AI: The Evolution of Artificial Intelligence

Artificial Intelligence, or AI, has become a ubiquitous term in our modern lexicon. From smartphones to smart homes, from customer service chatbots to autonomous vehicles, AI has permeated nearly every aspect of our lives. But how did we get here? The journey of AI from an obscure academic concept to a transformative force in society is a fascinating tale of human ingenuity, technological advancement, and evolving perceptions.

In this chapter, we'll explore the evolution of AI through three distinct phases: its technical beginnings, its portrayal in popular culture, and its current state of widespread accessibility. This journey not only illuminates the technological progress we've made but also reflects changing societal attitudes towards artificial intelligence. As we delve into each phase, we'll see how AI has moved from the exclusive domain of computer scientists and mathematicians to become a tool that's accessible to anyone with a smartphone or internet connection. This democratization of AI technology marks a significant shift in how we interact with and perceive intelligent machines.

Understanding this evolution is crucial for anyone looking to harness the power of AI, particularly in the realm of prompt engineering. By tracing AI's path from its roots to its current state, we can better appreciate the context in which we now create and interact with AI systems. This historical perspective will inform our approach to crafting effective prompts and working with AI tools.

So, let's embark on this journey through time, starting with the early days when AI was just a glimmer in the eyes of visionary computer scientists.

The Technical Beginnings

Early AI: A Programmer's Domain

The birth of artificial intelligence as a formal field of study can be traced back to the summer of 1956, at a workshop held at Dartmouth College. It was here that the term "Artificial Intelligence" was coined, and a group of visionary scientists laid the groundwork for what would become one of the most transformative technologies of our time.

In these early days, AI was firmly entrenched in the realm of academia and high-level computer science. The pioneers of AI were mathematicians, logicians, and computer scientists who saw the potential for machines to mimic human intelligence. Names like John McCarthy, Marvin Minsky, Allen Newell, and Herbert Simon became synonymous with the field, their work laying the foundation for decades of research to come.

The early focus of AI research was on solving problems that were intellectually challenging for humans but relatively straightforward for computers. This included tasks like playing chess, proving mathematical theorems, and solving logic puzzles. The approach was heavily rooted in symbolic AI, which attempted to represent human knowledge and reasoning processes using symbolic representations and rules.

Programming AI systems during this era was a complex and highly specialized task. It required not only advanced programming skills but also a deep understanding of cognitive science, logic, and mathematics. The languages used were often esoteric and purpose-built for AI research, such as LISP (List Processing) and Prolog (Programming in Logic).

These early AI systems were impressive in their own right. Programs like the General Problem Solver (GPS) developed by Newell and Simon could solve a wide range of well-defined problems. The ELIZA chatbot, created by Joseph Weizenbaum in 1966, could engage in seemingly intelligent conversation by using pattern matching and substitution methodology.

However, these systems also had significant limitations. They were brittle, meaning they could only operate within very narrow, predefined parameters. They lacked the ability to learn from experience or adapt to new situations, which are hallmarks of human intelligence. Moreover, they required enormous computational power by the standards of the time, often running on room-sized mainframe computers that were inaccessible to all but the most well-funded research institutions.

The 1970s and early 1980s saw the rise of expert systems, which attempted to capture the knowledge and decision-making processes of human experts in specific domains. While these systems found some success in narrow applications, they also highlighted the difficulties of encoding human knowledge and reasoning in a form that computers could use.

Throughout this period, AI remained firmly in the hands of specialists. The average person had little to no interaction with AI systems, and the field was viewed as an esoteric branch of computer science with little relevance to everyday life. The gap between the promise of AI and its practical applications in the real world was significant, leading to periods of reduced funding and interest known as "AI winters."

Despite these challenges, the foundational work done during this period was crucial. It established the theoretical frameworks and computational approaches that would later enable the AI revolution we're experiencing today. The dreams and ambitions of those early AI researchers, while perhaps overly optimistic in their timelines, set the stage for the remarkable AI capabilities we now take for granted.

As we'll see in the next section, while AI was making slow but steady progress in research labs, a very different vision of artificial intelligence was capturing the public imagination through the medium of popular culture.

The Gap Between AI and the General Public

While AI researchers were grappling with the complexities of creating intelligent machines, the general public remained largely unaware of these developments.

The highly technical nature of AI research, coupled with its confinement to academic and research settings, created a significant gap between the reality of AI and public perception.

For most people in the 1960s, 70s, and 80s, computers were distant, mysterious machines. The concept of a computer that could think or reason like a human was so far removed from everyday experience that it might as well have been science fiction. And indeed, for many, science fiction was the primary source of information about AI.

This disconnect between the actual state of AI technology and public understanding had several important consequences:

1. Misconceptions: Without access to accurate information about AI research, the public's understanding was often shaped by sensationalized media reports or science fiction. This led to widespread misconceptions about what AI could do and how it worked.

2. Unrealistic Expectations: The fantastic portrayals of AI in popular culture often created unrealistic expectations about the capabilities of AI systems. This contributed to cycles of hype and disappointment that plagued the field.

3. Fear and Skepticism: For some, the idea of intelligent machines evoked fear of job loss or even existential threats to humanity. These fears were often based on misunderstandings of the actual state and capabilities of AI technology.

31

4. Lack of Engagement: With AI perceived as a highly specialized, inaccessible field, there was little public engagement or discussion about the ethical and societal implications of AI development.

5. Limited Funding and Support: The esoteric nature of AI research made it difficult to garner widespread public or political support for funding, contributing to the "AI winters" when interest and investment in AI waned.

The technical language used by AI researchers further widened this gap. Terms like "neural networks," "heuristics," and "natural language processing" were meaningless to most people outside the field. Even when AI achievements were reported in the media, they were often framed in ways that emphasized their otherness – as curiosities of science rather than relevant developments that could impact everyday life.

Moreover, the lack of tangible AI products or services in the consumer space meant that most people had no direct experience with AI technology. Unlike other technological advancements of the time, such as personal computers or mobile phones, AI remained abstract and intangible to the average person.

This gap between AI reality and public perception would persist for decades. It would take the development of more user-friendly interfaces, the rise of the internet, and the integration of AI into everyday products and services to begin bridging this divide. As we'll explore in later sections, it's only in recent years that AI has truly entered the public consciousness as a technology that's relevant and accessible to everyone.

Understanding this historical gap is crucial for modern AI practitioners, particularly those working in prompt engineering. It reminds us of the importance of clear communication and accessible interfaces in making AI technology understandable and usable for a broad audience. As we craft prompts and design AI interactions, we must always be mindful of the end-user's perspective, working to bridge the gap between technical capability and user understanding.

In the next section, we'll explore how popular culture, particularly through films and literature, began to shape public perceptions of AI in ways that were often at odds with the reality of AI research but nonetheless influential in driving interest and speculation about the future of intelligent machines.

AI in Popular Culture

Imagine, for a moment, that you're a seed of an idea, planted in the fertile soil of human imagination. As you grow, you're not just shaped by the sunlight of scientific progress, but also by the colorful winds of popular culture. This is the journey of AI in our collective consciousness - a journey that has been as much about chrome-plated dreams as it has been about silicon chips and algorithms.

Hollywood's Vision: Robots and Superhumans

In the garden of public perception, Hollywood has been a master gardener, cultivating vivid and often fantastical images of what AI could be. These cinematic visions have been like vibrant flowers, captivating our attention and coloring our understanding of AI's potential.

Remember the first time you saw a robot on screen? Perhaps it was the dutiful R2-D2 from Star Wars, beeping and whirring its way into our hearts. Or maybe it was the menacing red eye of HAL 9000 in 2001: A Space Odyssey, its calm voice sending chills down your spine. These artificial beings, whether helpful or horrifying, planted seeds of wonder in our minds. What if machines could think, feel, and act like us - or even beyond us?

Hollywood's AI wasn't confined to humanoid shapes, though. Sometimes it was an all-seeing, all-knowing presence, like the computer in Star Trek that could answer any question with a mere "Computer, analyze." Other times, it was an entire simulated world, as in The Thirteenth Floor or eXistenZ, where reality itself became a playground for artificial minds.

These silver screen AIs were like exotic plants in our mental garden - beautiful, fascinating, but often bearing little resemblance to their real-world counterparts. They could learn, adapt, and grow at incredible speeds. They had personalities, desires, even souls. In short, they were everything that real AI wasn't - at least, not yet.

But here's the thing about seeds in a garden - they don't just grow on their own. They interact with their environment, and sometimes, they change it. Hollywood's AI didn't just entertain us; it shaped our expectations, our hopes, and our fears about what AI could become.

Think about it. How many times have you heard someone compare a new AI development to Skynet from Terminator? Or wonder if we're living in a simulation like The Matrix? These aren't just pop culture references - they're the fertilizer that's been feeding our understanding of AI for decades.

And like any good fertilizer, this mix of fact and fiction has both nourished and sometimes overstimulated our ideas about AI. It's made us dream big about the potential of intelligent machines. But it's also sown seeds of anxiety about a future where AI might outgrow its makers.

So, as we tend to our garden of knowledge about AI, we need to recognize these Hollywood visions for what they are - not as weeds to be uprooted, but as colorful blooms that add vibrancy to our understanding. They may not always reflect reality, but they've certainly shaped it. And who knows? Maybe some of those far-fetched sci-fi ideas will one day bear fruit in the real world of AI.

The Terminator, The Matrix, and Public Perception

Now, let's zoom in on two particularly influential flowers in our garden of AI perception: The Terminator and The Matrix. These cinematic juggernauts didn't just entertain us; they fundamentally altered the landscape of how we think about AI.

The Terminator series planted a seed of fear in our collective psyche. It painted a future where AI, in its relentless pursuit of efficiency, decides that humanity itself is the problem to be solved. The image of Arnold Schwarzenegger's relentless cyborg, with its glowing red eyes and metallic endoskeleton, became a vivid symbol of AI gone wrong. It was like a thorny rose in our garden - beautiful in its complexity, but with sharp edges that made us wary.

36

On the other hand, The Matrix offered a different, equally unsettling vision. Here, AI didn't just conquer humanity; it subjugated us in a virtual world of its own making. This was like a beautiful but parasitic vine, entwining itself around our understanding of reality and technology. The idea that our entire world could be a simulation created by machines struck a chord with ancient philosophical questions about the nature of reality.

These films didn't just tell stories; they asked profound questions. What is consciousness? What makes us human? Can machines ever truly think or feel? And if they can, what does that mean for us? These questions were like seeds of their own, taking root in the public consciousness and sprouting new thoughts and debates.

But here's where it gets interesting. While these films were painting AI as a potential existential threat, the real-world AI was quietly growing in a very different direction. It wasn't building Terminators or Matrix-style simulations. Instead, it was learning to recognize speech, to play chess, to help doctors diagnose diseases. The Hollywood AI was a towering oak, imposing and attention-grabbing. The real AI was more like a field of wheat - less dramatic, perhaps, but ultimately more nourishing for society.

This disconnect between perception and reality is like the difference between a perfectly manicured garden in a movie and the sometimes messy, always complex reality of an actual garden. Both have their place, but we need to understand the difference.

The impact of these films on public perception can't be overstated. They've become shorthand for our hopes and fears about AI. When a new AI breakthrough is announced, how often do we see headlines asking if Skynet is becoming real? Or jokes about whether we're living in the Matrix? These references aren't just pop culture footnotes - they're the lenses through which many people view AI developments.

This cinematic legacy presents both challenges and opportunities for those of us working in AI. On one hand, it means we're often fighting against preconceptions and fears that don't match the reality of our work. On the other hand, it means there's a deep well of public interest and engagement with AI concepts. People may come to AI with visions of Terminators in their heads, but that initial spark of interest can be nurtured into a more nuanced understanding.

As we continue to cultivate the field of AI, we need to be aware of these cultural influences. They're part of the soil in which we're growing this technology. We can't ignore them, but we can work to enrich that soil with more diverse, accurate, and balanced perspectives.

In the end, the AI of popular culture and the AI of reality are like two different species of plants in our garden of knowledge. Both have their place, and both contribute to the richness of our understanding. Our job is to appreciate the beauty and influence of the Hollywood visions while also tending carefully to the real-world AI saplings that are quietly growing into world-changing technologies.

So, the next time you watch a sci-fi film about AI, enjoy it for what it is. But also take a moment to look beyond the silver screen and see the real AI that's blooming all around us. It might not be as flashy as a Terminator, but in its own way, it's every bit as revolutionary.

AI Now: The Dawn of the Agentic Age

The Rise of Digital Co-workers: The Agentic World

The hype around chatbots is old news. The real revolution of 2025 is **agentic AI**, a paradigm Gartner has named the top tech trend of the year. An agentic AI is an autonomous system that can plan, reason, and act to complete complex tasks with minimal human oversight. Think of the difference between a calculator and a personal financial assistant. The calculator is a reactive tool; it waits for your command. The agentic assistant is proactive; it analyzes your goals, devises a plan, and executes it, perhaps by moving funds, paying bills, and generating a report.

This leap from reactive to proactive is powered by four key capabilities :

Planning: Breaking down complex, high-level goals into a series of smaller, actionable steps.

Reasoning: Thinking through problems logically to make decisions and adapt the plan as needed.

Memory: Remembering past interactions and learning from them to improve future performance.

Action: Executing tasks, using tools, and interacting with digital and even physical systems.

This shift is so fundamental that it requires a new way of thinking about AI architecture. We are moving from isolated, single-model applications to an **agentic AI mesh**—an interconnected network of specialized agents that collaborate to achieve complex organizational goals. Imagine a marketing campaign orchestrated not by a single person, but by a team of AI agents: one for market research, another for content creation, a third for ad placement, and a fourth for performance analytics, all working in concert. This node-based approach, where different agents are orchestrated to perform enterprise-wide workflows, is the foundation of the new "cognitive enterprise".

This new agentic world is already taking root. In customer service, AI agents are handling support tickets from start to finish. In sales, they are qualifying leads and scheduling meetings. In operations, they are monitoring systems and fixing issues before a human is even aware of a problem. This isn't a distant future; Deloitte predicts that 25% of companies using generative AI will launch agentic pilots in 2025, a number expected to double by 2027.

A Toolkit of Superpowers: Specialized AI in 2025

The rise of agentic AI has been accompanied by an explosion of powerful, specialized tools that act as the hands and feet for these new digital minds. These tools are no longer just general-purpose assistants; they are becoming masters of specific domains.

Deep Research: A prime example of agentic AI in action is the emergence of Deep Research tools. This capability allows an AI to take a complex query, autonomously break it down into discrete research tasks, scour hundreds of sources across the web (including text, PDFs, and images), and synthesize the findings into a structured, fully-cited report. Tools from OpenAI (powered by its o3 model), Google (Gemini Deep Research), and Perplexity are transforming a process that once took days of manual work into a task completed in minutes, making expert-level research accessible to everyone.

The AI Co-Engineer: The world of software development is being completely reshaped. We've moved beyond simple code completion to full-fledged AI co-engineers.

Cursor AI is an AI-first code editor that functions as a true partner in the development process. Its "Agent" mode can understand the entire codebase, debug errors, refactor multiple files, and execute complex tasks from end to end.

Lovable.dev takes this a step further, acting as a text-to-app platform. By simply describing an application in natural language, a user can generate a fully functional, full-stack app with a frontend, backend, and database, making rapid prototyping more accessible than ever.

Google AI Studio has become a comprehensive workspace for developers, integrating the powerful Gemini 2.5 Pro model directly into a native code editor and offering agentic tools like a new version of Colab that can autonomously execute tasks within a notebook.

The AI Filmmaker: The creative sphere has seen similar specialization. In a significant 2025 release, **Google's Veo 3** became globally available, offering a powerful text-to-video model that can generate 4K video clips complete with native audio, sound effects, and dialogue. This tool, alongside competitors like Kling, Seedance, OpenAI's Sora and Runway, represents another specialized superpower being added to the creative professional's toolkit.

The Screenless Future and Hyper-Personalization

As these powerful capabilities become more integrated, the very way we interact with AI is changing. The trend is moving toward **hyper-personalization** and a **"zero interface"** or **screenless future**. AI is no longer a destination we visit on a website or app; it's being woven into the fabric of our most-used applications, from AI-powered features in WhatsApp to deep search integration in Google.

Looking ahead, visionaries like OpenAI's Sam Altman and former Apple designer Jony Ive are exploring dedicated AI hardware that moves beyond the screen. The goal is to create an AI companion that experiences the world alongside us, blending technology so seamlessly into our routines that the interface effectively disappears. This is the ultimate expression of the democratization of AI—not just a tool you use, but an ever-present, intelligent partner in your daily life.

This journey from room-sized mainframes to autonomous digital co-workers has been nothing short of miraculous. And the most exciting part? The seeds of the agentic age are just beginning to sprout. The garden of possibilities is vaster than ever, and we are all its gardeners.

The Winds of Change: AI's Impact on Society

Imagine standing in our now-familiar AI garden, feeling a sudden gust of wind. It rustles the leaves, bends the stems, and carries seeds to new grounds. This wind is the transformative power of AI, sweeping across our societal landscape, reshaping industries, redefining jobs, and reimagining our very way of life.

This wind of change isn't a gentle breeze - it's a gale force that's uprooting old structures and scattering the seeds of innovation far and wide. It's exhilarating and terrifying, full of promise and peril. Like all significant changes, it brings both opportunities and challenges.

In this section, we'll explore how AI is reshaping our world. We'll look at the industries being transformed, the new possibilities emerging, and the potential pitfalls we need to navigate. But more than that, we'll discuss how we can not just weather this storm of change, but harness its power to propel us towards a better future.

Remember, in the face of this AI whirlwind, we're not helpless leaves being blown about. We're the gardeners, the innovators, the adapters. We have the power to bend with the wind, to plant new ideas, and to cultivate a future where AI and humanity flourish together.

So, let's unfurl our sails and see where these winds of change might take us.

The Importance of Embracing Change

Change, dear reader, is the only constant in life. It's the seasons in our AI garden, the shifting winds that keep our world dynamic and alive. But let's be honest - change can be scary. It's like stepping out of a cozy, familiar greenhouse into the wild, unpredictable outdoors.

This fear of change is deeply human. We're creatures of habit, finding comfort in routine and predictability. But in the face of AI's rapid advancement, clinging to the familiar is like trying to hold onto a tree in a hurricane - it might feel safe for a moment, but it won't serve us in the long run.

Let's take a moment to visit a cheese shop - not a real one, mind you, but the allegorical one from Dr. Spencer Johnson's famous book, "Who Moved My Cheese?"

In this tale, four characters live in a maze and rely on cheese for sustenance. One day, they discover their cheese supply has moved. Two mice, Sniff and Scurry, immediately set out to find new cheese. But two little people, Hem and Haw, resist the change, wondering, "Who moved my cheese?" Haw eventually realizes the futility of resisting and sets out, leaving behind messages like, "If you do not change, you can become extinct".

This little story about cheese is really about all of us in the face of change, especially the massive changes brought about by AI. In the world of AI, the cheese isn't just moving; it's constantly transforming. Yesterday's cheddar is today's blue cheese and might be tomorrow's entirely new dairy product we haven't even imagined yet.

Embracing change in the AI era isn't just about finding new cheese - it's about learning to make cheese ourselves, or maybe even discovering entirely new forms of sustenance.

Consider the professions that AI is already impacting. If you're a translator, AI isn't just moving your cheese - it's learning to translate faster and more accurately than ever before. If you're an artist, AI isn't just relocating your studio - it's picking up a brush and creating art itself.

But here's where our garden metaphor comes back into play. When the wind of change blows through a forest, it doesn't just knock things down - it also spreads seeds, creating opportunities for new growth. Those who embrace change are like the plants that bend with the wind, adapting to new conditions and finding ways to thrive.

For translators, AI can be a tool to handle routine tasks, freeing them to focus on the nuanced, culturally sensitive aspects of language that AI still struggles with. For artists, AI can be a new medium, a collaborator, or a source of inspiration, pushing the boundaries of creativity in unprecedented ways.

Embracing change means seeing AI not as a threat, but as a powerful new tool in our gardening kit. It's about asking, "How can I use this to grow something new and beautiful?" rather than lamenting the landscape that's shifting around us.

But embracing change isn't just about survival - it's about growth, innovation, and unlocking potential we never knew we had. When we embrace change, we become active participants in shaping the future, rather than passive observers being swept along by the tide of progress.

Think of embracing AI-driven change as embarking on an exciting expedition. Sure, you might have to leave your comfortable camp, but think of the new vistas you'll see, the new skills you'll learn, the new 'cheese' you'll discover!

Here are some practical steps to embrace the AI-driven change:

1. Stay curious: Like Sniff in our cheese story, keep your nose to the ground. Stay informed about AI developments in your field and beyond.

2. Be proactive: Like Scurry, don't wait for change to force your hand. Experiment with AI tools, even if they're not perfect yet. You'll be ahead of the curve when they improve.

3. Cultivate adaptability: Make learning a habit. The more flexible your skill set, the better you'll weather changes.

4. Focus on uniquely human skills: Emotional intelligence, creativity, ethical reasoning - cultivate the gardens that AI can complement but not replace.

5. Collaborate with AI: Don't think of it as "AI vs. humans," but "AI with humans." How can you use AI to enhance your work and life?

6. Embrace a growth mindset: Believe in your ability to learn and adapt. Your skills are not fixed, but constantly evolving.

7. Be the change: Don't just adapt to change - create it. Use AI to bring your innovative ideas to life.

Remember, in the story, it was Haw who wrote, *"The quicker you let go of old cheese, the sooner you find new cheese."* In our AI-driven world, the quicker we embrace change, the sooner we'll discover amazing new opportunities.

So, as the winds of AI-driven change blow through our garden of possibilities, don't be the rigid oak that breaks in the storm. Be the flexible reed that dances with the wind, adapting, growing, and thriving in this new, dynamic landscape.

After all, who knows? The cheese you find - or create - might be far more delicious than anything you've tasted before. The future is not something that happens to us - it's something we create. So let's embrace this change, and together, cultivate a future where AI helps our human potential bloom like never before.

Historical Parallels: Transformative Technologies

As we navigate the swirling winds of AI-driven change, it's worth glancing back at the weather patterns of the past. Our AI revolution isn't the first storm to reshape the landscape of human society. Let's explore some of the tempests that came before, and see what we can learn from those who weathered them.

The Computer Revolution

Imagine, if you will, a world where computers were as rare as exotic orchids, tended only by specialists in climate-controlled rooms. This was the reality not so long ago. But then came a revolution that would plant the seeds of personal computing in homes and offices around the world.

At the heart of this revolution were visionaries who saw potential where others saw complexity. They were like master gardeners, able to envision a flourishing ecosystem where others saw only circuitry and code.

Take Steve Jobs and Steve Wozniak of Apple, for instance. They weren't content with computers being the domain of big businesses and universities. They dreamed of a personal computer in every home, as common as a television set. With the Apple II, they planted a seed that would grow into a tech empire. Jobs, with his keen eye for design and user experience, understood that computers needed to be not just functional, but beautiful and intuitive. He was cultivating not just technology, but a relationship between humans and machines.

Meanwhile, Bill Gates and Paul Allen were sowing their own seeds at Microsoft. Their vision? Software that could run on any computer, creating a common language for these new electronic gardens. Windows would eventually become the soil in which countless software applications would grow, democratizing computing for millions.

But let's not forget the fertile ground these visionaries grew from. Xerox's Palo Alto Research Center (PARC) was like a hidden greenhouse, nurturing innovations that would change computing forever. The graphical user interface, the mouse, ethernet networking - these were all cultivated at PARC. Though Xerox didn't bring these innovations to market themselves, their ideas cross-pollinated the wider tech world, influencing both Apple and Microsoft.

And what of IBM, the original giant of the computing world? They were like an ancient, established forest, suddenly finding saplings of personal computers sprouting at their feet. Their response? The IBM PC, which set standards that would shape the industry for decades. It was as if the old forest had learned to produce new seeds, adapting to the changing climate of technology.

This revolution wasn't just about the machines themselves, but about how they changed our world. Computers went from being intimidating monoliths to friendly desktop companions. They became tools for creativity, productivity, and connection. The internet, itself born from this revolution, would turn these personal computers into windows to the world.

As we stand in our current AI garden, let's remember the lessons of the computer revolution. Innovation often comes from unexpected places. Visionaries see potential where others see obstacles. And sometimes, the most profound changes come not from the technology itself, but from how it reshapes our relationship with the world around us.

Digital Photography and Photoshop

Now, let's develop another snapshot of technological transformation - the revolution of digital photography and image editing. This shift was like changing the very soil in which visual creativity grew, transforming a world of chemicals and darkrooms into one of pixels and software.

Remember the days of film photography? Each shot was precious, a potential masterpiece hidden in the dark cocoon of a film canister. The process of developing photos was almost alchemical - in the red-lit mystery of a darkroom, images would slowly emerge from negatives, like butterflies unfurling their wings.

This process was an art form in itself, requiring skill, patience, and a touch of magic. Photographers were like gardeners tending to delicate plants, carefully controlling light, temperature, and chemical baths to coax their images into bloom.

But then came the digital revolution, sweeping through the photographic landscape like a change of seasons. Suddenly, the patience of waiting for film to develop was replaced by the instant gratification of digital previews. The limiting factor of 24 or 36 exposures per roll exploded into memory cards that could hold thousands of images.

At the forefront of this revolution was Adobe Photoshop, a tool that would redefine the boundaries of image manipulation. Photoshop was like a master gardener's toolkit, allowing artists to prune, graft, and cultivate images in ways never before possible. Blemishes could be erased, colors could be adjusted, and entire elements could be added or removed with a few clicks.

This digital revolution sent shockwaves through multiple industries. Let's focus our lens on a few:

In the world of animation and graphics, companies like Disney found themselves at a crossroads. Traditional hand-drawn animation, a painstaking frame-by-frame process, was suddenly competing with the efficiency and flexibility of computer-generated imagery (CGI). Movies like Toy Story bloomed in this new digital soil, showing the world the potential of fully computer-animated films.

But it wasn't just about creating new types of images - digital tools also transformed how we worked with existing ones. In the newspaper and magazine industry, the process of creating ads and laying out pages underwent a seismic shift. Gone were the days of physically cutting and pasting elements onto a board. Instead, designers could now compose entire pages digitally, adjusting layouts with ease and previewing changes instantly.

The film industry, too, found new creative freedom in these digital tools. Visual effects that once required painstaking practical work could now be achieved more easily (and often more convincingly) with CGI. Films like Jurassic Park showcased the potential of blending digital effects seamlessly with live action, planting the seeds for a new era of cinematic possibilities.

For the average person, digital photography and editing tools democratized image creation and manipulation. Suddenly, anyone with a digital camera (and soon, a smartphone) could capture high-quality images. Programs like Photoshop Elements brought powerful editing tools to home users, allowing everyone to enhance their photos, create digital scrapbooks, or experiment with graphic design.

This democratization had profound effects. On one hand, it unleashed a tidal wave of creativity, allowing more people than ever to express themselves visually. On the other hand, it raised new questions about the authenticity of images in a world where any photo could be easily altered.

The rise of social media platforms, particularly visually-focused ones like Instagram, further amplified the impact of these tools. Suddenly, everyone was a photographer, a curator of their own visual identity. Filters and editing tools became part of everyday life, changing how we present ourselves and perceive others.

In the professional world, the lines between different visual arts began to blur. Photographers could now offer retouching services. Graphic designers could incorporate photographic elements more easily into their work. And a new breed of digital artists emerged, creating works that defied traditional categorization.

As with any revolution, there were those who resisted. Some photographers clung to film, valuing its unique qualities and the discipline it required. There were (and still are) debates about the soul of photography - does the ease of digital detract from the art form? Is an unedited photo more "real" than one that's been retouched?

But for most, the benefits outweighed the nostalgia. The ability to take hundreds of shots without worrying about film costs allowed for more experimentation. The instant feedback of a digital camera helped photographers learn and improve more quickly. And the power of editing tools allowed for a level of control and creativity that was previously unimaginable.

As we reflect on this digital imaging revolution, we can see many parallels with our current AI transformation. Both represent a fundamental shift in how we create and interact with information. Both democratized powerful tools, putting capabilities once reserved for professionals into the hands of everyday users. And both raised important questions about authenticity, skill, and the nature of creativity in an increasingly technological world.

In our AI garden, we're seeing similar patterns. AI art generators are doing for visual creation what Photoshop did for photo editing - opening up new realms of possibility, blurring lines between disciplines, and challenging our notions of authorship and creativity.

So as we cultivate our AI tools, let's remember the lessons from the digital imaging revolution. Embrace the new possibilities, but don't forget the fundamental skills and artistic vision that give these tools meaning. And always be ready to adapt, for in the world of technology, the only constant is change.

How These Changes Reshaped Industries and Lifestyles

As we've seen, the computer revolution and the digital imaging transformation were not isolated events. They were more like changes in climate, fundamentally altering the ecosystem of our society. Let's take a moment to survey the landscape and see how these technological shifts reshaped our world.

In the realm of industry, these changes were like a rapid evolution, forcing businesses to adapt or face extinction. The rise of personal computers and digital tools reshaped office environments. Typewriters gave way to word processors, paper ledgers to spreadsheets, physical filing cabinets to digital databases. This wasn't just a change in tools, but in how work itself was structured and performed.

Industries that once relied heavily on physical processes found themselves in a new digital reality. Publishing, for instance, saw its entire workflow transformed. From authors writing on computers instead of typewriters, to editors using digital markup tools, to the rise of e-books and print-on-demand services - every stage of book creation and distribution was touched by this digital wind.

The music industry, too, found itself in a whirlwind of change. Digital recording techniques allowed for unprecedented control and manipulation of sound. CDs replaced vinyl and cassettes, only to be themselves disrupted by MP3s and streaming services. Artists could now record, produce, and distribute their music without ever leaving their home studios.

Retail and commerce underwent their own revolution. E-commerce platforms allowed businesses to reach customers around the globe, while digital inventory systems and data analytics tools transformed how companies managed their operations. The rise of digital marketing and social media created new ways for businesses to connect with consumers.

But these changes weren't confined to the world of work. They seeped into our personal lives, reshaping how we live, learn, and interact. Personal computers and the internet transformed homes into hubs of information and entertainment. Distance learning became a reality, opening up educational opportunities regardless of geographic location.

Digital cameras and smartphones turned everyone into a potential photographer or videographer, changing how we capture and share our lives. Social media platforms, built on these digital foundations, rewired our social connections and communication patterns.

Even our leisure activities felt the impact. Video games, evolving from simple pixels to complex digital worlds, became a major entertainment industry. Streaming services, enabled by digital video technology and high-speed internet, revolutionized how we consume movies and TV shows.

These changes also brought new challenges. The digital divide became a pressing issue, as access to these technologies increasingly determined one's opportunities in the modern world. Concerns about privacy and data security entered the public consciousness. The rapid pace of change led to generational gaps in technological literacy.

Yet for all the challenges, these changes also brought tremendous opportunities. They democratized access to information and tools of creation. They allowed for new forms of collaboration and connection across vast distances. They enabled innovations that improved healthcare, education, and quality of life for millions.

As we stand in our current AI garden, we can see echoes of these past revolutions. Once again, we're seeing tools that were once the domain of specialists becoming accessible to all. We're witnessing the blurring of lines between human and machine capabilities. And we're grappling with the profound ethical and societal implications of these changes.

The lessons from these past transformations are clear. Adaptability is key. Those who embrace change and learn to leverage new tools will thrive. But it's also crucial to guide these changes with wisdom and foresight, considering their broader impacts on society.

As we cultivate AI technologies, let's remember that their true power lies not in the tools themselves, but in how we use them to enhance our human capabilities, to solve pressing problems, and to create a better world for all. The seeds of the future are in our hands. What kind of garden shall we grow?

AI: The Next Big Shift

As we stand in our garden of technological marvels, a new season is upon us. The winds of change are blowing once again, carrying the seeds of artificial intelligence far and wide. This isn't just a new tool sprouting in our garden - it's a fundamental shift in the very soil beneath our feet. This shift is fueled by an unprecedented "arms race" for technological supremacy.

The scale of investment is staggering: Meta has earmarked $65 billion for AI in 2025, including a plan for 1.3 million GPUs and a data center the size of a significant part of Manhattan; Microsoft has committed $80 billion for its AI data centers; and there are reports of a $500 billion "Project Stargate" initiative involving OpenAI and other major players. This massive injection of capital and resources explains the frantic pace of innovation and has direct consequences for every creative professional, as it shapes the very tools we use daily.

Industry-wide Transformations in Action

The impact of this AI-driven shift is no longer a prediction; it is a reality unfolding across every sector. The seeds planted by AI research are now bearing fruit in tangible, world-altering applications.

In **healthcare and pharmaceuticals**, the transformation is profound. In a landmark development, AI-designed drugs have entered human trials, marking a new era in medicine. This is not an isolated event. Pharma Global Capability Centers (GCCs) are now routinely using AI to drastically cut the time and cost of drug development, employing models for molecule prediction and clinical trial simulation. On the diagnostic front, new AI models are demonstrating over 90% accuracy in the early detection of diseases like cancer by analyzing patient history, imaging, and biomarkers, a breakthrough with the potential to revolutionize preventive care.

The world of **science and materials** is also being reshaped. In a clear demonstration of AI's problem-solving power, scientists have used it to develop a novel eco-friendly paint formula that can significantly cool buildings by reflecting solar radiation. The AI accelerated the material discovery process, identifying ideal compounds in a matter of days—a task that would have traditionally taken years. This is a major victory for sustainable architecture and green technology.

In the corporate world of **business and finance**, the abstract concept of AI is giving way to concrete, value-generating tools. Agentic platforms, which combine multiple AI tools to automate complex workflows, are being deployed at scale. For example, Banco BV, a major Brazilian bank, is using Google's Agentspace platform to allow employees to discover, connect, and automate tasks across its vast data systems securely. Similarly, consultancies like Deloitte are using these platforms to bridge data silos and foster rapid experimentation, with AI even identifying connections in reports that human analysts had missed. This "silo busting" is empowering a wider range of users within organizations to participate in AI-driven innovation.

The New Fabric of Daily Life

The changes are not confined to large-scale industries; they are altering the very fabric of our daily work and personal lives, weaving AI into the mundane and the magnificent. The "AI co-worker" is no longer a futuristic concept but a present-day reality, fundamentally changing how we approach creativity, productivity, and collaboration.

The Creative Partner: From Ideation to Final Polish The creative process for many has been transformed. It often begins with **ideation**, where professionals and hobbyists alike use LLMs like ChatGPT or Claude as tireless brainstorming partners. A marketing manager might prompt an AI to generate five unique campaign concepts for a new product, while a student might ask for three different thesis statements for an essay.

This partnership continues into **content creation**. An initial draft of a blog post, a social media update, or even a complex report can be generated in seconds. But the AI's role doesn't end there. It then transforms into a sophisticated **proofreader**, checking for grammar and spelling, but also suggesting stylistic improvements, adjusting the tone for a specific audience, and ensuring clarity. This iterative loop of generation and refinement accelerates the writing process immensely.

The same revolution is happening in visual arts. **Image creation** tools like Midjourney are no longer just for professional artists. A project manager can now generate custom images for a presentation, a small business owner can create unique visuals for their social media feed, and a teacher can produce illustrations for a lesson plan, all with a simple text prompt.

The Automated Assistant: Taming Daily Tasks Beyond creative pursuits, AI is automating a wide range of daily tasks. The nature of collaborative work is changing with features like ChatGPT's `Record Mode`, which can listen to a meeting, transcribe it, and then automatically generate a summary, a list of action items, and even draft follow-up emails. This turns unstructured conversation into structured, actionable data, freeing up human participants to focus on the discussion itself.

The true power of this new era lies in **collaboration between different tools**, orchestrated by the user. A content creator's workflow might now look like this:

Ideation & Scripting: Use Claude to brainstorm a video concept and write a script.

Visuals: Use Midjourney V7 to generate a series of high-quality storyboard images based on the script's scene descriptions.

Animation: Import those images into a tool like Runway Gen-4 to animate them, adding motion and life.

Music: Generate a custom background score using SUNO to match the video's mood.

This multi-tool approach, where the user acts as an "AI Orchestrator," is becoming increasingly common. It's further enhanced by features like ChatGPT's `Connectors`, which allow the AI to access and synthesize information from disparate sources like Google Drive and HubSpot, automating the creation of complex reports that draw on multiple data streams.

The Human-AI Relationship and Its Complexities
This rapid integration of AI is a two-sided coin. While productivity is soaring, the relationship between humans and AI is growing more nuanced and complex. Scientists have developed AI models that can predict human decision-making in complex moral and social dilemmas with surprising accuracy, raising profound questions about the nature of judgment and the potential for AI to act as an ethical sounding board.

At the same time, there are growing concerns about the potential erosion of fundamental human skills. This tension is acutely visible in education, where the use of tools like ChatGPT has led to a rampant cheating problem, forcing institutions to grapple with how to leverage AI's benefits without hindering the development of critical thinking and deep understanding. This presents a practical dilemma for every individual and organization: how do we harness the incredible efficiency gains offered by AI without undermining the core competencies that have always been the bedrock of human progress?

Societal and Legal Guardrails Finally, the societal and legal landscape is racing to catch up to the technology. The proliferation of generative AI has led to tangible legal responses. In a significant move, the United States passed the "Take It Down Act" in May 2025, making the creation and distribution of nonconsensual AI-generated deepfake imagery a federal crime. This reflects a growing societal pushback against the misuse of these powerful tools and signals the beginning of a new era of legal and ethical guardrails designed to manage AI's integration into the very fabric of our lives.

Visualizing with AI: Developing AI as a Skill

Imagine, for a moment, that you're standing at the edge of a vast, uncharted ocean. This ocean is artificial intelligence - deep, complex, and full of potential. Many people view AI as a boat, a tool to help them navigate this ocean. They climb aboard, push a few buttons, and expect to be carried to their destination. But here's the thing: AI isn't just a boat. It's the ocean itself, ever-changing and full of currents, depths, and hidden treasures. To truly harness its power, we need to learn to swim.

This is why we need to think of AI not just as a tool, but as a skill to be developed. A tool is something you use; a skill is something you embody. A tool can be picked up and put down; a skill becomes a part of you, shaping how you think and interact with the world.

Consider the difference between someone who occasionally uses a map app to navigate, and a seasoned explorer who can read the stars, interpret terrain, and intuitively sense direction. The app user can get from point A to point B, sure. But the explorer? They can chart new courses, understand the landscape on a deeper level, and adapt to unexpected changes. That's the difference between using AI as a tool and developing AI as a skill.

Developing AI as a skill means going beyond surface-level interactions. It's not just about knowing which buttons to push or prompts to type. It's about understanding the underlying principles, recognizing patterns, and developing an intuition for how AI systems think and work. It's about learning to communicate with AI in a way that leverages its strengths while compensating for its weaknesses.

Moreover, as AI continues to evolve at a breakneck pace, treating it as a fixed tool will quickly leave you behind. Today's cutting-edge AI application might be obsolete tomorrow. But if you've developed AI as a skill, you'll be able to adapt quickly, applying your understanding to new systems and applications as they emerge.

Think of it this way: learning to use a specific AI tool is like learning a phrase in a foreign language. It's useful, but limited. Developing AI as a skill is like becoming fluent in that language. You can express complex ideas, understand nuances, and even create new expressions. You're not just using the language; you're thinking in it.

As we dive deeper into this ocean of AI, we'll explore how to cultivate this skill, how to develop an AI mindset that will serve you well no matter how the technology evolves. We'll learn to swim in these digital waters, navigating currents of data, diving into depths of algorithms, and surfacing with insights and creations that were once unimaginable.

So, are you ready to go beyond the boat and learn to swim in the AI ocean? Let's dive in.

Beyond Tools: Cultivating an AI Mindset

Picture a master chef in a kitchen. They're not just following recipes or using utensils. They understand flavors at a molecular level, they can predict how ingredients will interact, they can improvise and create new dishes on the fly. That's the difference between using cooking tools and having a culinary mindset. Now, let's apply that same concept to AI.

Cultivating an AI mindset means developing a deep, intuitive understanding of how AI systems work, think, and interact with the world. It's about seeing the world through an AI's "eyes" (or rather, its algorithms), understanding its strengths and limitations, and learning to communicate with it effectively.

Let's break this down with a story.

Meet Sarah, a graphic designer. When she first encountered AI tools like Emagen 4, Gpt-Image or Midjourney, she approached them like any other design software. She'd type in a description, get an image, and either use it or discard it. The results were hit-or-miss, and she often felt frustrated when the AI didn't produce exactly what she had in mind.

But then Sarah decided to dive deeper. She started learning about how these AI models were trained, how they interpreted text prompts, and how they generated images. She began to see patterns in what kinds of descriptions led to better results. She learned that AI models have their own "language" of sorts, and she needed to learn to speak it.

Over time, Sarah developed what we might call an "AI mindset." She no longer saw the AI as just a tool to generate images, but as a collaborative partner in the creative process. She learned to "think like the AI" when crafting her prompts. She understood that vague descriptions like "beautiful landscape" would yield generic results, while specific, vivid descriptions with contextual details would produce more unique and tailored images.

Sarah also learned to work with the AI's quirks and limitations. She realized that these models sometimes struggled with certain concepts like hands or text, so she learned to break complex ideas into simpler components the AI could handle better. She began to see the AI's "mistakes" not as failures, but as opportunities for unexpected creativity.

This mindset shift transformed Sarah's work. She was no longer just using AI to generate images; she was engaging in a dance of human and artificial creativity, each playing to their strengths. Her prompts became more like conversations with the AI, guiding it towards her vision while remaining open to its interpretations.

But cultivating an AI mindset goes beyond just getting better results from AI tools. It's about developing a new way of thinking that can be applied across various domains and AI applications. Let's explore some key aspects of this mindset:

1. Systems Thinking: AI systems are complex and interconnected. An AI mindset involves understanding how different parts of a system interact, how input affects output, and how changing one variable can have ripple effects throughout the system.

2. Pattern Recognition: AI excels at finding patterns in data. Developing an AI mindset means honing your own pattern recognition skills, learning to see connections and trends that might not be immediately obvious.

3. Probabilistic Thinking: AI doesn't deal in certainties, but in probabilities. An AI mindset involves getting comfortable with uncertainty and thinking in terms of likelihoods rather than absolutes.

4. Data Awareness: AI runs on data. An AI mindset involves being constantly aware of the data around us, understanding its value, and thinking about how it can be collected, processed, and utilized.

5. Iterative Improvement: AI models learn through repeated iterations. An AI mindset embraces this iterative approach, valuing continuous improvement and learning from each attempt.

6. Ethical Consideration: As AI becomes more powerful, ethical considerations become increasingly important. An AI mindset involves constantly considering the ethical implications of AI applications and striving for responsible use.

Developing this mindset doesn't happen overnight. It's a gradual process of learning, experimenting, and reflecting. It involves staying curious, being willing to make mistakes, and constantly pushing the boundaries of what you think is possible.

Let's go back to Sarah for a moment. As she developed her AI mindset, she found it influencing areas of her life beyond just her design work. She began to approach problems differently, breaking them down into data points and patterns. She became more comfortable with ambiguity and more adept at navigating complex systems. She found herself better able to communicate complex ideas, having practiced distilling concepts into clear, AI-friendly prompts.

Cultivating an AI mindset is not about replacing human thinking with machine thinking. It's about developing a new set of mental tools that complement and enhance our uniquely human capabilities. It's about learning to dance with AI, each partner playing to their strengths to create something greater than either could achieve alone.

As we continue to navigate this AI-infused world, developing this mindset will become increasingly valuable. It will allow us to adapt to new AI technologies as they emerge, to use AI more effectively in our work and daily lives, and to shape the development of AI in ways that benefit humanity.

So, as you embark on your journey of developing AI as a skill, remember: it's not just about learning to use AI tools. It's about cultivating a new way of thinking, a new way of seeing the world. It's about developing an AI mindset that will serve you well no matter how the technology evolves. Are you ready to start thinking differently?

Thinking Like AI: Different Approaches

Imagine your mind as a vast, multifaceted gemstone. Each facet represents a different way of thinking, a unique approach to viewing and interacting with the world. When we're crafting prompts for AI, we're essentially trying to align these facets of our mind with the AI's way of processing information. It's like finding the right angle to catch the light, making our gemstone of thought shine its brightest.

In this chapter, we'll explore three main facets of this gemstone: literal thinking, lateral thinking, and technical thinking. Each of these approaches offers a unique way to communicate with AI, whether you're a writer weaving stories, a programmer building digital architectures, an artist painting with pixels, or someone navigating AI in a non-native language.

Remember, the key here isn't just about writing prompts – it's about cultivating a mindset, about learning to think in ways that resonate with AI. It's about developing the power of visualization, of seeing in your mind's eye what you want the AI to create, and then finding the best way to translate that vision into words.

So, let's polish each facet of our thinking gemstone and see how it can help us shine in the world of AI prompting.

Literal Thinking and Writing

Literal thinking is like looking at the world through a clear, unfiltered lens. It's about taking things at face value, being direct and precise in your communication. When it comes to AI prompting, literal thinking can be incredibly powerful, especially when you need the AI to follow specific instructions or generate concrete, factual content.

Let's explore this with some examples:

Writer's Mindset:

Imagine you're a novelist wanting to describe a specific scene. In your mind, you see a sunlit beach with golden sand and turquoise waves. Here's how you might approach this with literal thinking:

1. Visualize: See the beach in your mind's eye. What exactly do you see?

2. Describe precisely: *"Create an image of a beach with golden yellow sand. The ocean should be turquoise blue. The sun is high in the sky, casting short shadows."*

This literal description gives the AI clear, concrete elements to work with.

Programmer's Mindset:

As a programmer, you often need to give precise instructions. Let's say you're using AI to help with coding. You might think:

1. Visualize: Picture the structure and function of the code you need.

2. Describe logically: *"Write a Python function that takes two parameters: a list of integers and a target sum. The function should return a tuple of two numbers from the list that add up to the target sum. If no such pair exists, return None."*

This literal, step-by-step thinking translates well to both coding and instructing AI.

Artist's Mindset:

For visual artists, literal thinking can help in describing specific elements of an artwork. Imagine you're creating a still life:

1. Visualize: See the arrangement of objects in your mind.

2. Describe concretely: *"Generate an image of a still life composition. Include a red apple, a blue ceramic vase, and a silver spoon on a wooden table. The lighting should be coming from the left side."*

This literal description ensures each element is clearly represented.

For Non-Native English Speakers:

If English isn't your first language, literal thinking can be your ally. Focus on simple, clear descriptions:

1. Visualize: Picture what you want, focusing on basic elements.

2. Describe simply: *"Make picture of house. House is big. House is white. House has red roof. Tree is next to house."*

Even with simple language, this literal description can yield effective results.

The key with literal thinking is precision and clarity. It's about translating what you see in your mind into clear, unambiguous language. This approach works well when you need the AI to follow specific instructions or create something with well-defined elements.

Lateral Thinking and Writing

Lateral thinking is like looking at the world through a prism, seeing how different ideas can connect in unexpected ways. It's about creativity, making unusual associations, and thinking outside the box. When prompting AI, lateral thinking can lead to unique, innovative outputs, especially useful for brainstorming, creative writing, and generating novel ideas.

Let's explore this approach:

Writer's Mindset:

Imagine you're a science fiction author wanting to create a unique alien world. Here's how you might use lateral thinking:

1. Visualize: Instead of picturing a typical planet, imagine unexpected combinations. What if the planet was alive? What if time flowed differently there?

2. Describe creatively: *"Create a story setting on a sentient planet where time flows like water, pooling in some areas and rushing in others. The inhabitants have evolved to surf these time currents."*

This lateral approach combines unrelated concepts (planet, sentience, time, water) to create something novel.

Programmer's Mindset:

As a programmer, lateral thinking can help solve problems in innovative ways. Let's say you're using AI to brainstorm a new app idea:

1. Visualize: Think of combining seemingly unrelated concepts. What if a fitness app was also a plant-growing game?

2. Describe imaginatively: *"Design a mobile app concept that gamifies fitness by linking users' physical activity to the growth of a virtual forest. Each completed workout nurtures and expands the user's digital ecosystem."*

This merges fitness tracking with virtual gardening, potentially creating a unique motivational tool.

Artist's Mindset:

For artists, lateral thinking can spark surreal and thought-provoking creations. Imagine you're creating a piece about climate change:

1. Visualize: Think metaphorically. How can you represent climate change in an unexpected way?

2. Describe metaphorically: *"Generate an image of a giant hourglass. The top half contains a lush forest and blue skies, while the bottom half shows a desert with a red, hazy sky. Instead of sand, trees are falling through the hourglass's neck."*

This uses the familiar image of an hourglass in an unexpected way to represent a complex issue.

For Non-Native English Speakers:

Lateral thinking can actually be liberating if you're not fluent in English. Focus on connecting simple ideas in unusual ways:

1. Visualize: Think of combining basic concepts in new ways.

2. Describe creatively: *"Make picture of fish swimming in sky. Birds swimming in ocean. Sun is blue. Moon is green."*

Even with limited vocabulary, this lateral approach can yield interesting, surreal results.

The key with lateral thinking is to make unexpected connections. It's about looking at familiar things in new ways and combining ideas that don't usually go together. This approach is particularly useful when you want the AI to generate creative, original content or help with out-of-the-box problem-solving.

Technical Thinking and Writing

Technical thinking is like viewing the world through a microscope, focusing on details, processes, and precise specifications. It's about understanding and describing how things work, often using specialized language. When prompting AI, technical thinking is crucial for tasks that require specific expertise, detailed instructions, or when working within particular domains like science, engineering, or technology.

Let's explore this approach:

Writer's Mindset:

Even for writers, technical thinking can be valuable, especially when crafting detailed world-building or writing about specialized topics. Imagine you're writing a hard science fiction novel about space travel:

1. Visualize: Picture the spacecraft in detail. How does it work? What are its specifications?

2. Describe technically: *"Design a schematic for an interstellar spacecraft. The ship should use a fusion drive for propulsion, have a rotating habitat ring for artificial gravity (diameter: 200 meters, rotation: 2 rpm), and employ a magnetic field for radiation shielding. Include details on life support systems and long-term cryostasis pods."*

This technical approach ensures accuracy and depth in your world-building.

Programmer's Mindset:

For programmers, technical thinking is often second nature. When using AI for coding tasks, this approach is crucial:

1. Visualize: Think in terms of system architecture, data flows, and algorithms.

2. Describe technically: *"Create a UML diagram for a microservices architecture. The system should include services for user authentication, data processing, and API gateway. Use REST for inter-service communication and implement OAuth 2.0 for security. Include a message queue for asynchronous tasks and a caching layer for improved performance."*

This detailed, technical prompt gives the AI specific parameters to work with.

Artist's Mindset:

For visual artists, especially those working with AI image generation, technical thinking involves understanding and specifying the precise details of image creation. Let's reimagine you're a photographer or cinematographer wanting to create a specific scene:

1. Visualize: Think about the technical aspects of the shot - camera settings, lighting, composition, and post-processing.

2. Describe technically: Use the following template, filling in the bracketed sections with your specific details:

"Generate an image of [scene description] captured with a [camera type] using a [lens type] lens at [focal length]mm. Set the aperture to f/[aperture number] for [desired depth of field effect], with a shutter speed of [shutter speed] to [desired motion effect]. Use ISO [ISO number] for [desired noise level]. Compose the shot using [composition technique], with the [main subject] positioned [subject position]. The lighting should be [lighting condition] with the main light source [light source position]. Set the color temperature to [color temperature]K for a [warm/cool] tone. Include [additional elements or effects] in the scene. In post-processing, apply [post-processing technique] to enhance [desired enhancement]. The overall style should be [artistic style]."

This technical approach provides a flexible template that can be adapted for various photographic or cinematographic scenarios, giving specific parameters that an AI can use to generate or edit an image, mimicking the level of control a photographer would have in a real shoot.

Technical thinking can be particularly helpful for non-native English speakers, as it allows you to focus on specific, universal concepts and terminology. Whether you're writing or creating images, this approach can help you communicate your ideas effectively.

For Writing:

Visualize: Focus on the structure and style of your writing.

Describe technically: Use the following template, filling in the bracketed sections with your specific details:

"Create a [type of text: e.g., article, story, essay] about [main topic]. Use a [formal/informal/neutral] tone. The text should be [number] words long. Structure it with [number] paragraphs. Include an introduction, [number] main points, and a conclusion. Use [simple/complex] sentence structures. The vocabulary level should be [basic/intermediate/advanced]. Include [number] technical terms related to [field or topic]. Use [active/passive] voice predominantly. The writing style should be [descriptive/narrative/persuasive/expository]. Add [metaphors/similes/other literary devices] to enhance the writing."

For Image Creation:

Visualize: Think about the composition and technical aspects of the image you want to create.

Describe technically: Use the following template, filling in the bracketed sections with your specific details:

"Generate an image of [main subject] in a [setting/location]. The image should be [horizontal/vertical] with a [wide/medium/close-up] shot. Position the main subject in the [position in frame: e.g., center, left third, bottom right]. Use [type of lighting: e.g., natural, studio, high contrast] lighting from the [direction] side. The color scheme should be [warm/cool/neutral/vibrant]. Include [background elements] in the scene. The mood of the image should be [describe mood: e.g., cheerful, somber, energetic]. Use a [shallow/deep] depth of field to [blur/keep in focus] the background. Add [any special effects or filters] to the image."

These templates provide a structured way to think about and describe your writing or image creation goals, focusing on technical aspects that are universal and less dependent on advanced language skills. By filling in the bracketed sections, you can create detailed, technical prompts that communicate your vision effectively to AI tools, even if you're not fully fluent in English.

Even with simple language, this technical approach conveys complex information effectively.

The key with technical thinking is precision and detail. It's about breaking complex systems or processes into clear, specific components. This approach is particularly useful when you need the AI to generate or work with specialized, detailed information, or when accuracy and specificity are crucial.

Remember, these thinking styles - literal, lateral, and technical - aren't mutually exclusive. The most effective AI prompts often combine elements of each. The skill lies in knowing when to use which approach, and how to blend them for optimal results. As you practice these different ways of thinking, you'll develop a more nuanced, flexible approach to crafting AI prompts, enabling you to communicate your ideas more effectively regardless of your background or the task at hand.

Da Sachin Sharma

Synthesizing Approaches for Optimal Results

Imagine you're a chef in a gourmet kitchen. You have a variety of ingredients (literal thinking), a flair for unique flavor combinations (lateral thinking), and a deep understanding of cooking techniques (technical thinking). The magic happens when you blend these elements, creating dishes that are both precisely crafted and innovatively delicious. This is the art of synthesizing different thinking approaches when working with AI.

Just as a master chef doesn't rely solely on following recipes, measuring ingredients, or creative improvisation, but rather combines all these skills, so too should we aim to synthesize our different thinking approaches when crafting AI prompts. Let's explore how to do this effectively.

The Power of Synthesis

Synthesizing different thinking approaches allows us to create prompts that are simultaneously precise, creative, and technically sound. This combination can lead to AI outputs that are not only accurate and detailed but also innovative and tailored to our specific needs.

Let's break down how we can combine our three thinking styles:

1. Literal + Lateral: This combination allows for clear, specific instructions (literal) while encouraging unexpected connections or outcomes (lateral). It's particularly useful for creative tasks that still require some structure.

2. Literal + Technical: This synthesis provides precise, detailed instructions (literal) with domain-specific language and parameters (technical). It's ideal for specialized tasks that require accuracy and expertise.

3. Lateral + Technical: This blend encourages innovative thinking within a technical framework. It's great for problem-solving in specialized fields or pushing the boundaries of what's possible within certain technical constraints.

4. Literal + Lateral + Technical: The ultimate synthesis, combining all three approaches, can lead to prompts that are clear, creative, and technically sophisticated.

Let's look at some examples of how this synthesis might work in practice.

Writing a Sci-Fi Story

Imagine you're using AI to help write a science fiction story about time travel. Here's how you might synthesize different thinking approaches:

1. Literal Thinking: "Write a 500-word story about a scientist who invents a time machine."

2. Lateral Thinking: "Imagine time as a physical substance that can be manipulated like clay."

3. Technical Thinking: "Include accurate references to quantum mechanics and the theory of relativity."

Synthesized Prompt:

"Create a 500-word science fiction story about a scientist who discovers that time is a tangible, clay-like substance that can be molded and shaped. The scientist invents a device that can manipulate this 'time-clay,' effectively creating a time machine. Incorporate accurate references to quantum mechanics and the theory of relativity to explain how the device works. The story should explore the personal and ethical dilemmas the scientist faces when they realize they can change

history. Use vivid, sensory language to describe the experience of molding time and traveling through it. The narrative should have a clear beginning, middle, and end, with a surprising twist that challenges the reader's perception of cause and effect."

This synthesized prompt combines the clear structure from literal thinking, the creative concept from lateral thinking, and the scientific accuracy from technical thinking.

Generating a Marketing Visual

Let's say you're using AI to create a visual for a marketing campaign about sustainable technology. Here's how you might combine approaches:

1. Literal Thinking: *"Create an image of a green energy technology product in use."*

2. Lateral Thinking: *"Show the product as a living entity that grows and evolves."*

3. Technical Thinking: "Use specific photography techniques to enhance the visual impact."

Synthesized Prompt:

"Generate an image for a sustainable technology marketing campaign. The main subject should be a solar panel array, but visualize it as a living, growing entity. Show the solar panels as leaves or petals of a giant, futuristic flower blooming on a hillside. The image should be a wide-angle shot (24mm equivalent) with a deep depth of field (f/11) to keep both the 'solar flower' and its environment in focus. Use golden hour lighting coming from the left side to create a warm, hopeful atmosphere. The color palette should emphasize greens and golds. Incorporate a subtle motion blur effect (1/15 sec shutter speed) on some elements to suggest growth and change. In the background, include a city skyline transitioning from grey, polluted buildings on one side to clean, green architecture on the other, symbolizing the transformation enabled by the technology. Apply HDR techniques in post-processing to ensure both shadow detail in the solar panels and highlight detail in the sky are visible. The overall style should be photorealistic with a touch of surrealism."

This synthesized prompt combines a clear description of the desired elements (literal), an innovative concept of technology as a living entity (lateral), and specific photographic and post-processing techniques (technical).

Coding a Unique Algorithm

Suppose you're using AI to help design a new algorithm for data analysis. Here's how you might blend the thinking styles:

1. Literal Thinking: *"Create a Python function for analyzing financial data."*

2. Lateral Thinking: *"Imagine the data analysis process as an ecosystem where different types of data interact like species in a food web."*

3. Technical Thinking: *"Incorporate advanced statistical methods and machine learning techniques."*

Synthesized Prompt:

"Design a Python function for financial data analysis that models the analysis process as an ecological system. The function should take as input a pandas DataFrame containing various financial metrics (e.g., stock prices, volume, P/E ratios) over time.

Treat each financial metric as a 'species' in the ecosystem. The interactions between these 'species' should be modeled using techniques inspired by ecological concepts such as predator-prey relationships, symbiosis, and competition. For example, high trading volume might be a 'predator' that affects stock price volatility.

Implement the following technical components:
1. Use a combination of time series analysis (ARIMA models) and machine learning techniques (Random Forests for feature importance).
2. Incorporate a Monte Carlo simulation to model the stochastic nature of the 'ecosystem'.
3. Implement a custom loss function that balances predictive accuracy with the 'health' of the overall ecosystem (e.g., maintaining diversity of influential factors).

The function should output:
1. Predictions for future values of key metrics.
2. A visualization of the 'ecosystem', showing the relationships between different financial 'species'.
3. An interpretability report explaining how different factors influence each other and the overall system.

Ensure the code is well-documented, follows PEP 8 standards, and includes unit tests for each major component. Optimize the function for performance, considering the use of NumPy for numerical operations and parallel processing for the Monte Carlo simulations."

This synthesized prompt combines a clear description of the desired function (literal), an innovative conceptual framework (lateral), and specific technical requirements and methodologies (technical).

The Art of Synthesis

Synthesizing these approaches is not about using them all equally in every prompt. Rather, it's about understanding when and how to blend them for optimal results. Here are some tips:

1. Start with a clear goal (literal thinking) to ground your prompt.

2. Use lateral thinking to add unique angles or solve problems creatively.

3. Apply technical thinking to add depth, accuracy, and specificity.

4. Iterate and refine. Your first synthesized prompt may not be perfect, and that's okay. Adjust the balance of approaches based on the AI's output.

5. Practice, practice, practice. The more you work with these different thinking styles, the more naturally you'll be able to synthesize them.

Remember, the goal is not to create the longest or most complex prompt possible. It's to craft a prompt that communicates your vision clearly and effectively to the AI, balancing precision, creativity, and technical depth as needed for your specific task.

By mastering this synthesis, you'll be able to craft prompts that push the boundaries of what AI can do, whether you're writing, coding, creating visual art, or tackling complex analytical tasks. Like our master chef, you'll develop an intuition for when to measure precisely, when to add a creative twist, and when to apply advanced techniques – all in service of creating something truly remarkable.

Understanding LLMs and Prompting for LLMs: Cultivating Conversations with Artificial Intelligence

Imagine, for a moment, that you're standing at the entrance of a vast, magical garden. This garden is unlike any you've seen before – it's a living, breathing ecosystem of knowledge, capable of growing and shaping itself in response to your words. This, dear reader, is the world of Large Language Models (LLMs), and you are the gardener, armed with the tools of prompting to cultivate this digital landscape.

The fundamental shift from 2024 to 2025 is that this is no longer a single, peaceful garden. It has erupted into a battlefield, a great "LLM War" where established giants and disruptive newcomers clash, each cultivating highly specialized and powerful new species of AI. The art of prompting has evolved. It's no longer just about crafting the perfect seed for one type of soil. It's about understanding which faction in this war—which specialized AI model—is best suited for the task at hand. The modern creative professional is less of a simple gardener and more of an expert botanist and battlefield strategist, an "AI Orchestrator," who must strategically choose the right weapon for each specific task to achieve victory.

The Art of Prompting: Planting Seeds of Conversation

Just as a gardener must understand the nuances of different plants, we must first grasp the various styles of prompting. Each method is like a different type of seed, capable of growing into unique conversational flora when planted in the fertile soil of an LLM.

One-Shot Prompting: The Quick-Bloom Annual One-shot prompting is like planting a fast-growing annual. You provide a single example or instruction, and the LLM responds based on that alone. It's quick, direct, and can yield impressive results, but it may lack the depth of more complex methods.

Example: Human: "Translate 'Hello, world' to French." AI: "Bonjour, le monde."

Few-Shot Prompting: The Perennial Bed Few-shot prompting is akin to planting a bed of perennials. You provide multiple examples, allowing the LLM to recognize patterns and apply them to new situations. This method often results in more consistent and nuanced outputs.

Example: Human: "Translate the following to pirate speak: 'Hello, my friend!' -> 'Ahoy, me hearty!' 'Where is

101

the treasure?' -> 'Where be the booty?' 'Let's go on an adventure.' ->?" AI: "Let's set sail for adventure, arrr!"

Chain-of-Thought Prompting: The Climbing Vine

Chain-of-thought prompting is like nurturing a climbing vine. You encourage the LLM to "think aloud," showing its reasoning process step-by-step. This method is particularly useful for complex problem-solving tasks, as it forces the model to break down the problem before arriving at a conclusion, often leading to more accurate results.

Example:

Human: "Q: Roger has 5 tennis balls. He buys 2 more cans of tennis balls. Each can has 3 tennis balls. How many tennis balls does he have now?

A: Roger started with 5 balls. 2 cans of 3 tennis balls each is 2 * 3 = 6 balls. 5 + 6 = 11. The answer is 11.

Q: The cafeteria had 23 apples. If they used 20 to make lunch and bought 6 more, how many apples do they have?

A:" AI: "The cafeteria started with 23 apples. They used 20, so they had 23 - 20 = 3 apples. They bought 6 more, so they now have 3 + 6 = 9 apples. The answer is 9."

How LLMs Work: Growing a Digital Mind

Now, let's delve into how these marvelous digital gardens grow and flourish. The journey of an LLM is not unlike the growth of a human mind – it starts small, absorbs vast amounts of information, and gradually learns to make sense of it all.

The process begins with training data, a massive corpus of text and code from the internet, books, and other sources. This is the rich soil from which the LLM will grow. Through a process involving complex neural networks, the model learns to recognize patterns in this data. It develops "roots" that connect words and concepts, understanding semantic relationships. It learns grammar and sentence structure, which act as the "stem," providing a framework for more complex knowledge. Finally, it develops the ability to understand context—the "leaves" that turn towards the sun—and eventually "blooms" with the ability to generate new, coherent, and creative text.

The Art of Crafting Briefs: Tending to Your AI Garden

Now that we understand the nature of our AI garden, let's explore how to tend it effectively. Crafting a good brief is like providing the right care for your plants – it's essential for healthy growth and beautiful results.

Step 1: The Greeting - Planting the Seed Just as you wouldn't start gardening without first stepping into the garden, always begin your interaction with a greeting. A simple "Hi" or "Hello" sets the tone for a respectful and productive conversation.

Step 2: Setting the Role - Choosing Your Plant Next, consider what type of "plant" you want to grow. Are you looking for a technical expert, a creative writer, or perhaps a friendly tutor? Specify the role you want the LLM to take on.

Example: "Act as a seasoned travel blogger specializing in budget travel in Southeast Asia."

Step 3: Clarifying the Task - Providing Nutrients Just as plants need specific nutrients to thrive, LLMs need clear information to produce the best results. If you're not sure how to provide all the details, don't worry – the LLM can ask questions to clarify the task.

Example: "Help me plan a 3-week itinerary. I'm interested in culture, food, and nature. My budget is $1500."

Step 4: Refining the Output - Pruning and Shaping Like a gardener who prunes and shapes plants for optimal growth, you can refine the LLM's output through feedback and additional prompts. Don't be afraid to ask for revisions or expansions on certain points.

Example: "That's a great start. Can you replace the trip to the elephant sanctuary with a recommendation for a local cooking class in Chiang Mai?"

The 2025 LLM Arena: A Guide to the Great AI War

Welcome, AI Orchestrator, to the front lines of the Great AI War of 2025. The once-peaceful garden of language models has transformed into a fiercely contested battlefield. Tech titans, nimble startups, and new regional powers are locked in a relentless arms race, each deploying increasingly specialized and powerful models. To thrive, you must understand the strengths and weaknesses of each faction's arsenal.

The Incumbent Powers: The Big Four

The established giants continue to innovate, moving away from one-size-fits-all models to entire families of specialized AI.

OpenAI's Specialized Suite: OpenAI has diversified its lineup, offering a model for every need and budget.

GPT-4o: The versatile flagship, excelling at creative tasks and general use.

GPT-4.1: The developer's powerhouse, with a massive context window for complex coding and document analysis.

o3: The logic and reasoning engine, designed for scientific, mathematical, and strategic planning tasks.

Anthropic's Differentiated Pair: Anthropic offers two powerful models, each with distinct strengths.

Claude 4 Opus: Their frontier model, leading the pack in complex coding and agentic problem-solving.

Claude 4 Sonnet: A balanced and efficient workhorse, ideal for enterprise-scale deployment and powering tools like GitHub Copilot.

Google's Integrated Family: Google's strategy centers on a deeply integrated family of models.

Gemini 2.5 (Pro, Flash, Flash-Lite): A tiered family offering different balances of speed, capability, and cost, powering advanced features like the "AI Mode" in Google Search.

Meta's Open-Source Offensive: Backed by a colossal $65 billion investment, Meta is championing the open-source movement.

Llama 4: The next generation of their open-source model, aimed at competing with the best proprietary systems and democratizing access to frontier AI.

Meta Superintelligence Labs: A new division poaching top talent, signaling their ambition to achieve Artificial General Intelligence (AGI).

The Disruptors: New Challengers Reshaping the Battlefield

The dominance of the incumbents is being challenged by new players with revolutionary approaches.

The DeepSeek Revolution: In early 2025, a little-known Chinese startup named DeepSeek sent shockwaves through the industry. They achieved performance comparable to top-tier models at a fraction of the cost, challenging the long-held belief that cutting-edge AI requires billion-dollar investments. Their key innovation is the

Mixture-of-Experts (MoE) architecture, which activates only the necessary "expert" parts of the model for a given task, drastically reducing computational costs. By open-sourcing their models, DeepSeek has ignited a new wave of accessible AI development, proving that efficiency and optimization can be as powerful as brute-force investment.

Groq: The Speed Specialist: Groq is not an LLM developer but a crucial hardware innovator. They have developed the **Language Processing Unit (LPU)**, a chip designed specifically for AI inference—the process of running a trained model. The LPU delivers unparalleled speed and low latency, allowing models like Llama and Mixtral to run faster than on traditional GPUs. By providing this "inference-as-a-service," Groq is becoming the go-to infrastructure for developers who need real-time AI responses, establishing data centers globally to meet demand.

The Indian AI Uprising

Recognizing the need for AI that understands its unique linguistic and cultural landscape, India has emerged as a new AI power.

SUTRA by TWO AI: Founded by renowned innovator Pranav Mistry, TWO AI launched SUTRA, a groundbreaking multilingual model supporting over 50 languages. Its unique

dual-transformer architecture decouples conceptual understanding from language processing, making it incredibly efficient and cost-effective for non-English languages like Hindi, Gujarati, and Korean. For these languages, SUTRA can be up to 8 times more token-efficient than English-centric models, dramatically lowering the cost of use. The free chatbot, ChatSUTRA, makes these capabilities widely accessible.

Sarvam AI: Backed by the Indian government's IndiaAI Mission, Sarvam AI is developing sovereign LLMs tailored for India. Their models, including the 24-billion parameter

Sarvam-M, are built on open-source foundations like Mistral and fine-tuned for exceptional performance in Indian languages, mathematics, and coding. They are designed to understand the unique way Indians mix English and local languages ("Hinglish"), a nuance often lost on other models.

Tending the Digital Garden: Working with LLM APIs

The evolution of LLMs has been accompanied by a parallel evolution in how we interact with them. Beyond simple chat interfaces, Application Programming Interfaces (APIs) and new agentic capabilities allow for deeper integration and more complex automation.

ChatGPT Connectors: Your Personal Data Analyst
A significant 2025 development for ChatGPT is the rollout of `Connectors`. This feature allows users to link their ChatGPT to personal and enterprise data sources like Google Drive, Dropbox, Microsoft SharePoint, and more. This transforms the AI from a general knowledge engine into a powerful personal data analyst. A user can now craft prompts that instruct the AI to perform tasks on their own data.

Example Prompt: "Using the connected Q2 sales reports in my Dropbox folder, identify the top three performing product categories by revenue, calculate their growth percentage from Q1, and draft a summary email to the marketing team highlighting these successes."

Anthropic's Agentic API and Claude Code SDK

Anthropic has explicitly designed its new API capabilities to empower developers to build powerful AI agents. The Claude 4 API includes a `Files API` for interacting with documents, a `code execution tool` to run and test code, and prompt caching for efficiency.

The release of the `Claude Code SDK` and its native integration into popular Integrated Development Environments (IDEs) like VS Code and JetBrains, as well as on GitHub, represents a major leap for developers. This allows a programmer to use Claude as an intelligent pair programmer directly within their existing workflow. They can tag Claude on a pull request to respond to reviewer feedback or ask it to fix a bug, turning the AI into an active, collaborative team member.

Forging Your Digital Allies: Customizing AI Companions

The true power of the modern AI landscape lies not just in using these powerful models, but in shaping them to our specific needs. The leading AI platforms now offer robust tools for creating bespoke AI experiences, allowing you to move beyond the role of a simple user to become the architect of your own specialized digital assistants. Whether you're building a focused expert, an interactive workspace, or a long-term project collaborator, each platform provides a unique approach to AI customization.

OpenAI's Custom GPTs: The Specialist Gardener

Imagine being able to breed your own specialized AI gardener, one that's an expert in exactly the type of plants you're cultivating. This is the power of creating a Custom GPT. It allows you to tailor an AI's knowledge, personality, and capabilities to a specific purpose, creating a focused and highly effective assistant.

The creation process is an intuitive conversation with the GPT Builder. You start by defining your goal with a clear, descriptive prompt. For instance: "Let's create a GPT that is an expert in International Financial Reporting Standards (IFRS) and is designed to help accountants and auditors." The builder will then suggest a name, like "IFRS Insight," and even generate a profile picture using DALL-E.

The real customization happens in the "Configure" tab. Here, you can refine the AI's instructions, upload specific knowledge files (like PDFs of IFRS regulations), and select its capabilities, such as web browsing or image analysis. The most significant 2025 update is the ability to perform

Model Selection. This is a game-changer. You are no longer limited to a single engine. You can now choose the underlying model that best suits your custom AI's purpose.

For an "IFRS Insight" bot that needs to perform logical analysis of regulations, you would select **o3**, OpenAI's logic powerhouse.

For a creative writing partner designed to help brainstorm surrealist poetry, the versatile and imaginative **GPT-4o** would be the ideal choice.

For a coding assistant built to help debug large repositories, you would choose **GPT-4.1** for its massive context window.

This ability to match the AI's core "brain" to its intended function allows for a level of precision and effectiveness that was previously impossible, turning you into a true breeder of specialist AI companions.

Google's Custom Experiences: The AI Tinkerer's Workshop

Google's approach to customization is less about creating a distinct "bot" and more about building custom, interactive AI-powered experiences and applications. It's a tinkerer's workshop, providing powerful tools to weave AI directly into your workflow.

The **Gemini Canvas** is a prime example of this philosophy. It's an interactive, document-style workspace where generation and editing merge. You can use a prompt to generate a first draft of a report or a Python script, and then, instead of writing follow-up prompts for revisions, you can enter the Canvas and edit the text or code directly. This hybrid approach is incredibly powerful. You can highlight a specific paragraph and prompt the AI to "rewrite this section in a more formal tone," or select a function in your code and ask the AI to "review this block for potential errors and suggest an optimization." It transforms the interaction from a simple conversation into a dynamic collaboration on a shared document.

For building more standalone applications, **Google AI Studio** is your go-to tool. It's a browser-based environment where you can experiment with the latest Gemini models and, crucially, build and deploy custom no-code apps. You can create a "Live Persona Chat" that uses Gemini's real-time voice to let you talk to an ideal customer profile, or a "Contract Analyzer" that ingests legal documents and creates a visual dashboard of risks and key clauses. This is Google's answer to custom AI: not just a chatbot with a new personality, but a fully-fledged, purpose-built application powered by AI.

Anthropic's Claude Projects: The Long-Term Collaborator

Anthropic's Claude takes a different approach to customization, one focused on depth and persistence. Its unique **Projects** feature is like having a dedicated, intelligent greenhouse for each of your complex ideas.

Unlike a standard chat that resets its context, a Claude Project maintains the entire conversational history over long periods. This makes it an unparalleled tool for deep, long-term work. Think of it as a persistent, shared workspace between you and the AI. You can begin brainstorming a novel in one session, come back days later to ask Claude to summarize your main plot points, and then return the following week to start drafting a chapter, all without losing the thread of the conversation.

This makes Projects the ideal environment for tasks that require sustained focus and evolving context, such as:

In-depth Research: You can gather sources, ask Claude to summarize them, and build a complex analysis over time.

Writing a Book or Screenplay: The AI remembers your characters, plot points, and stylistic choices from one session to the next.

Developing a Business Plan: You can work through market research, financial projections, and strategic

117

planning iteratively, with the AI maintaining full context of your evolving plan.

Claude's approach is not about creating a disposable, single-purpose bot. It's about fostering a long-term intellectual partnership, making it the perfect customized companion for your most ambitious and complex endeavors.

Mastering the Art of AI Prompting: A Universal Guide

In the ever-evolving landscape of artificial intelligence, the ability to communicate effectively with AI models has become a cornerstone skill. The principles of prompting are no longer confined to a single platform like ChatGPT; they are a universal language for interacting with a diverse ecosystem of powerful models from Google, Anthropic, OpenAI, and others. Whether you are conversing with Gemini, collaborating on a long-term task in a Claude Project, or experiencing the near-instantaneous responses of a model running on Groq's lightning-fast hardware, the art of the prompt remains your key to unlocking the full potential of these digital minds.

This chapter will delve deep into the universal strategies and platform-specific tactics for effective AI prompting, providing you with the tools to elevate your interactions across the entire 2025 AI landscape.

The Universal Foundations of Effective Prompting

Before we dive into platform-specific techniques, it's crucial to understand the three pillars of effective prompting that apply to any advanced AI model. Think of these as the primary colors on your artistic palette; by blending them, you can create any shade of output you desire.

Literal Thinking: This is the foundation—clear, direct instructions that leave no room for misinterpretation. It's about precision and clarity.

Lateral Thinking: This is the creative spark—imaginative approaches that encourage unique, innovative, and unexpected outputs.

Technical Thinking: This is the fine-tuning—using specific parameters, constraints, and domain-specific language to shape the AI's response with expert control.

By mastering the synthesis of these three approaches, you can craft prompts that are simultaneously precise, creative, and technically sophisticated, regardless of the AI you are interacting with.

Six Core Strategies for Crafting Powerful Prompts (Across All Platforms)

These six strategies are fundamental tactics that will improve the quality of your results on any major LLM platform, from ChatGPT to Gemini to Claude.

Write Clear Instructions: An AI, for all its sophistication, cannot read your mind. The more explicit and detailed your instructions, the better the output.

Tactic: Adopt a Persona. Instructing the model to act as a specific expert *(e.g., "Act as a world-renowned physicist and explain quantum entanglement in simple terms")* primes it to respond with the appropriate tone, style, and depth of knowledge.

Provide Reference Text: When accuracy is paramount, ground the AI's response in facts. Providing source text for the model to draw from minimizes the risk of generating incorrect information, or "hallucinations."

Tactic: Instruct for Grounded Answers. Start your prompt with "Using the following text, answer the question below," followed by your reference material and then your question. This forces the model to base its answer on the information you've provided.

Split Complex Tasks into Simpler Subtasks: Just as a human would, AI models produce higher-quality work when a large, complex task is broken down into smaller, manageable steps.

Tactic: Sequential Prompting. Instead of asking for a complete 10-page report in one go, first ask for an outline. Then, in subsequent prompts, ask the AI to expand on each section of the outline one by one.

Give the Model Time to "Think": For problems that require reasoning, forcing the model to show its work before providing a final answer can dramatically improve accuracy. This is the core of chain-of-thought prompting.

Tactic: Instruct for Step-by-Step Solutions. Begin your prompt with, "First, work out your own solution to the problem step-by-step. Then, provide the final answer." This encourages a more logical and less error-prone reasoning process.

Use External Tools and Capabilities: Modern AI platforms are not isolated. They can browse the web, execute code, and, with new features like ChatGPT's `Connectors`, interact with your personal data sources.

Tactic: Leverage Code Execution for Accuracy. For mathematical calculations or data analysis, ask the model to write and execute Python code. This offloads the calculation to a reliable interpreter, ensuring accuracy.

Test Changes Systematically: To refine your prompting skills, you need a methodical way to evaluate outputs.

Tactic: Evaluate Against a "Gold Standard." Create a reference or "gold-standard" answer for a specific query. When you test a new prompt, compare the

AI's output to your reference answer to systematically measure improvement.

Putting It All into Practice: Prompt Formulas for Common Tasks

Understanding the strategies is one thing; applying them is another. For a first-time user, starting with a blank prompt can be intimidating. To make it simple, here are some easy-to-use formulas that combine these core strategies to help you tackle common professional and creative tasks. Think of these as recipes for success.

Formula 1: The Social Media Calendar

Goal: To get a structured, actionable content plan for your social media channels.

The Prompt Formula: *"Act as an expert [****]. Create a [****] social media content calendar for [****]* on **[Platform, e.g., Instagram]**.

The target audience is [****]. The brand's tone of voice is [****].

The main content pillars are:

Please provide the output in a table with the following columns: Day, Content Pillar, Post Idea, a sample Caption, and 3-5 relevant Hashtags."

Example in Action: *"Act as an expert **Social Media Strategist**. Create a **1-week** social media content calendar for **'EcoChic,' a sustainable fashion brand,** on **Instagram**.*

*The target audience is **urban professionals aged 25-40 who value style and environmental responsibility**. The brand's tone of voice is **sophisticated, inspiring, and conscious**.*

The main content pillars are:

Sustainability Spotlight

Style Inspiration

Community Feature

Please provide the output in a table with the following columns: Day, Content Pillar, Post Idea, a sample Caption, and 3-5 relevant Hashtags."

Why This Works: This prompt is effective because it uses a persona (Strategy 1), provides clear and detailed instructions (Strategy 1), and breaks down the content requirements into pillars (Strategy 3), guiding the AI to produce a well-organized and highly relevant calendar.

Formula 2: The Strategic Plan

Goal: To generate a comprehensive strategy document for a project or business.

The Prompt Formula: *"Act as a [****]. Develop a comprehensive marketing strategy for the launch of [****].*

Product Information: [****]

*The primary business goal is **[Your Goal, e.g., to achieve 10,000 users in the first quarter]**.*

Please structure the strategy with these specific sections:

Target Audience Persona: A detailed profile of the ideal customer.

Key Messaging: The core messages we want to communicate.

Recommended Marketing Channels: A list of the best platforms to reach our audience.

Launch Campaign Idea: A creative concept for the initial launch campaign.

Key Performance Indicators (KPIs): How we will measure success."

Example in Action*: "Act as a **Senior Marketing Strategist***. Develop a comprehensive marketing strategy for the launch of **'ConnectSphere,' a new AI-powered networking app**.

Product Information: 'ConnectSphere' uses AI to suggest meaningful professional connections based on a user's career goals, skills, and past projects, going beyond simple job titles. Its unique feature is an 'Icebreaker Generator' that provides personalized conversation starters for new connections.

*The primary business goal is **to achieve 50,000 downloads in the first 6 months***.

Please structure the strategy with these specific sections:

Target Audience Persona

Key Messaging

Recommended Marketing Channels

Launch Campaign Idea

Key Performance Indicators (KPIs)"

Why This Works: *This prompt excels by breaking a very complex task into five smaller, manageable subtasks (Strategy 3). It also provides essential reference text (Strategy 2) about the product, ensuring the AI's strategic recommendations are grounded and relevant.*

Formula 3: The Perfect Newsletter

Goal: To quickly draft an engaging and well-structured newsletter.

The Prompt Formula*: "You are a [****] for **[Your Company/Publication]**. Write a draft for our weekly newsletter.*

***Newsletter Topic:** [****] **Target Audience:** [****] **Tone:** [****]*

The newsletter must include:

*A catchy and short **Subject Line**.*

*A brief, personal **Introduction** that hooks the reader.*

*Three main points based on this information: **[Provide bullet points or a short paragraph of reference text for the AI to expand upon]**.*

*A clear **Call-to-Action** at the end, telling the reader to [****]."*

Example in Action: *"You are a **professional copywriter** for **'AI Insights Weekly'**. Write a draft for our weekly newsletter.*

Newsletter Topic: The rise of agentic AI in the workplace. Target Audience: Tech professionals and business leaders interested in AI trends. Tone: Informative, insightful, and slightly futuristic.

The newsletter must include:

A catchy and short **Subject Line**.

A brief, personal **Introduction** *that hooks the reader.*

Three main points based on this information: ***Agentic AI is Gartner's top tech trend for 2025. Unlike chatbots, agents can plan and execute tasks autonomously. Companies like Deloitte are already using them to automate complex workflows.***

A clear ***Call-to-Action*** *at the end, telling the reader to* ***read our full in-depth report on the blog."***

Why This Works: This formula provides the AI with clear constraints and reference material (Strategy 2), preventing it from going off-topic. By specifying the structure (intro, three points, CTA), you ensure the output is well-organized and serves its purpose effectively.

Prompting the Prompt: The Art of Meta-Prompting

Sometimes, the hardest part of getting a great result is knowing how to write the perfect prompt in the first place. This is where a powerful technique called **meta-prompting** comes in. You are essentially asking the AI to act as an expert prompt engineer for you.

Goal: To have the AI generate a high-quality, detailed prompt that you can then use to get the best possible output for a specific task.

The Meta-Prompt Formula*: "You are an expert Prompt Engineer for [****]. Your task is to create a detailed, expert-level prompt for me.*

My goal is to [****].

*Please generate a prompt that is optimized for [****] and includes all the necessary details, such as **[mention key elements like style, tone, format, technical details, etc.]**. The final prompt should be ready for me to copy and paste."*

Example 1: Getting a Prompt for Image Generation (Midjourney) *"You are an expert Prompt Engineer for **Midjourney V7**. Your task is to create a detailed, expert-level prompt for me.*

*My goal is to **create a photorealistic image of a futuristic, eco-friendly city where buildings are covered in lush greenery**.*

*Please generate a prompt that is optimized for **Midjourney V7** and includes all the necessary details, such as **subject, setting, composition, lighting, artistic style, and technical parameters like aspect ratio and stylization**. The final prompt should be ready for me to copy and paste."*

Example 2: Getting a Prompt for Video Creation (Runway) *"You are an expert Prompt Engineer for **Runway Gen-4**. Your task is to create a detailed, expert-level prompt for me.*

*My goal is to **create a short, cinematic video clip of a classic muscle car driving down a deserted highway at sunset**.*

*Please generate a prompt that is optimized for **Runway Gen-4** and includes all the necessary details, such as **camera movement, scene description, action, mood, and visual style**. The final prompt should be ready for me to copy and paste."*

Why This Works: This technique leverages the AI's own knowledge of what makes a good prompt. By assigning it the persona of a Prompt Engineer (Strategy 1) and giving it a clear goal and constraints (Strategy 1 & 3), you guide it to create a prompt that is far more detailed and effective than what you might have written yourself. It's the ultimate shortcut to becoming a power user.

Advanced Prompting: A Platform-Specific Guide for 2025

While the core principles are universal, the true AI Orchestrator knows how to adapt their prompting style to leverage the unique strengths and features of each platform.

Prompting for Interactive and Agentic Workflows (OpenAI & Google)

The paradigm is shifting from simple conversation to interactive collaboration. Platforms like OpenAI's ChatGPT and Google's AI Studio now feature interactive canvases and data connectors that require a new style of prompting focused on action and direct manipulation.

The Interactive Canvas (ChatGPT & Gemini): The `Canvas` feature in both ChatGPT and Google's Gemini allows you to directly edit a model's response or code block. This blends prompting with direct manipulation.

Strategy: Generate and Refine. Use an initial prompt to generate a draft (*e.g., "Draft a marketing plan for a new sustainable sneaker brand"*). Then, instead of writing a follow-up prompt to ask for changes, enter the `Canvas` and make edits directly. You can then highlight a specific section and use a targeted prompt like, *"Rewrite this* *paragraph in a more persuasive tone and add three supporting statistics.*"

Prompting with Data Connectors (ChatGPT): ChatGPT's `Connectors` are a powerful feature that allows the AI to securely access and synthesize information from your personal or enterprise data sources, like Google Drive, Dropbox, or HubSpot. This requires a new skill: prompting the AI to query your own data.

Strategy: Synthesize Across Sources. The true power is in synthesis. Craft prompts that ask the AI to draw information from multiple connected sources. For example: "*Review the customer feedback in my connected Gmail from the last 30 days and the sales data from the 'Q2_Sales.xlsx' file in my OneDrive. Identify the top three product complaints and correlate them with any dips in sales, then summarize the findings in a memo.*"

Live Prompting with `Record Mode` (ChatGPT): Available on the macOS desktop app, `Record Mode` transcribes and summarizes audio from meetings or voice notes, turning conversation into actionable outputs. This introduces "live prompting," where the structure of your conversation becomes the prompt.

Strategy: Structure Your Conversation. Begin meetings with a clear agenda and verbally assign action items (e.g., *"Okay, the action item for John is to research competitor pricing by Friday"*). This provides strong cues for the AI to accurately capture tasks and decisions.

Prompting for Speed and Real-Time Interaction (Models on Groq)

Groq has revolutionized AI interaction by focusing on hardware. Their custom-built Language Processing Units (LPUs) deliver unparalleled inference speed, allowing models like Llama and Mixtral to respond in near real-time. This low latency enables a completely different prompting style.

Strategy: Rapid-Fire Conversation. With Groq, you don't need to craft one perfect, long prompt. The minimal delay allows for a fluid, rapid back-and-forth conversation. You can ask a question, get an instant answer, and immediately ask a follow-up to refine or correct the output. This turns prompting into a high-speed iterative process, much like a natural human conversation.

Prompting for Deep Research (Google Gemini & OpenAI)

For complex research tasks, specialized "Deep Research" capabilities have emerged on platforms from Google and OpenAI. These agentic systems can take a high-level query, autonomously browse hundreds of web sources, and synthesize the findings into a structured, cited report.

Strategy: Crafting Multi-Layered Queries. These tools excel with complex, exploratory questions that would normally require dozens of separate searches. Instead of asking, "What is quantum computing?", a more effective prompt would be: "Provide a comprehensive overview of quantum computing, including its fundamental principles, the current state of hardware development, its potential impact on cryptography, and the key companies leading the research, supported by recent sources." This gives the AI agent a clear, multi-faceted research plan to execute.

By mastering these universal principles and platform-specific techniques, you move from simply conversing with an AI to directing a powerful, data-aware, and increasingly specialized team of digital assistants. The skill lies in understanding which tool to use for which task and how to craft your prompts to leverage their unique capabilities, solidifying your role as an effective AI Orchestrator in this new and exciting era.

Painting with Pixels: The Art of AI Image Creation

Welcome to the digital art studio of the future, a place where your words are the brush, your imagination is the palette, and artificial intelligence is your tireless, infinitely skilled artistic partner. The world of AI image creation has exploded into a vibrant, chaotic, and breathtakingly innovative scene. The quiet galleries of 2024, dominated by a few famous artists, have given way to a bustling 2025 metropolis of creativity, filled with grand ateliers, independent studios, and open-access workshops.

In this chapter, we will embark on a grand tour of this new artistic landscape. We'll visit the studios of the **flagship models**—the great masters like Midjourney, Google's Imagen 4, OpenAI's GPT-4o, and the revolutionary Flux—each with their own signature style. We'll also explore the world of **wrapper websites**, the accessible public galleries that make powerful AI tools available to everyone.

Most importantly, we will learn the craft itself. We'll move beyond simple descriptions to master the art of prompting, learning how to create consistent characters that can star in their own stories, how to train our own specialist AI artists using **LoRA models**, and even peek into the power user's workshop with an introduction to the node-based canvas of **ComfyUI**. Prepare to transform your ideas into visual masterpieces.

The Great AI Ateliers: A Tour of the 2025 Flagship Models

In the world of AI art, a few major studios, or "ateliers," set the standard for quality and innovation. These are the flagship models, developed by the largest AI labs, each offering a unique artistic sensibility.

Midjourney V7: The Cinematic Impressionist

Imagine an AI artist with the soul of a dramatic, impressionistic painter, capable of capturing the essence of your ideas in breathtaking strokes of digital light. This is Midjourney. Known for its beautiful, cinematic, and often painterly aesthetic, Midjourney has long been a favorite of AI artists and filmmakers.

With the release of **Version 7 (V7)** in early 2025, Midjourney rebuilt its entire system, resulting in a dramatic leap in quality. It now boasts a much stronger understanding of prompts, superior photorealism, and more precise detail. While it began its life exclusively on the chat platform Discord, it now has a more user-friendly web interface where you can craft your creations. Midjourney remains the master of mood and atmosphere, perfect for creating epic landscapes, ethereal portraits, and images that blur the line between a photograph and a dream.

Google's Imagen 4: The Photorealistic Powerhouse

If Midjourney is the impressionist, then Google's Imagen 4 is the master of photorealism. Integrated directly into Google's AI tools like Gemini and the standalone ImageFX experience, Imagen 4 excels at creating images with stunning clarity, intricate detail, and lifelike textures.

Where Imagen 4 truly pulls ahead of the competition is in its ability to render text. For years, AI models struggled to produce coherent words, but Imagen 4 can generate crisp, accurate typography, making it an invaluable tool for creating posters, logos, and infographics. It has an incredible eye for the fine details in a photograph—the texture of fabric, the glisten of water droplets, the individual strands of animal fur—making it the go-to choice when you need an image that is almost indistinguishable from reality.

OpenAI's GPT-4o Image Generation: The Conversational Creator

OpenAI, the creators of ChatGPT, have taken a different approach. Instead of a standalone image tool, they have woven image generation directly into the fabric of their flagship model, **GPT-4o**. This is the successor to the famous DALL-E series, and its strength lies in its conversational nature.

With GPT-4o, creating an image is a dialogue. You can ask for an image, and then refine it through conversation: "That's great, but can you make the sky a deeper shade of blue?" or "Now, add a small boat on the lake." It excels at following complex, multi-step instructions and can even use an uploaded image as a reference or starting point for a new creation. This makes GPT-4o a uniquely flexible and intuitive tool, turning the act of creation into a natural, collaborative chat with your AI assistant.

Flux: The Open-Weight Challenger

Emerging from Black Forest Labs—a studio founded by the original minds behind Stable Diffusion—Flux is a powerful and versatile new artist on the scene. As an "open-weight" model, it offers a powerful alternative to the closed systems of the other giants. Flux is renowned for its incredible prompt fidelity, meaning it does an excellent job of creating exactly what you describe.

Flux comes in several versions, including a lightning-fast "Schnell" model for rapid experimentation and a high-quality "Pro" model for finished works. It also features

Flux Kontext, a suite of tools that allows for in-context image editing, letting you modify existing images with simple text prompts. For those who value precision and control, Flux has quickly become a formidable and essential tool.

140

The Accessible Galleries: Understanding Wrapper Websites

While the flagship models are the grand ateliers, not everyone needs to commission a master painter for every task. This is where **wrapper websites** come in. Think of them as public galleries or community art studios. These are user-friendly websites that "wrap" a powerful, often open-source AI model (like Stable Diffusion or Flux) in an easy-to-use interface, frequently with a free tier.

These platforms make AI image generation accessible to everyone, regardless of technical skill. They often add their own unique features on top of the core model, such as:

Playground AI: A popular platform that offers a generous free plan and simple design tools to edit your creations, remove backgrounds, or upscale images.

Recraft: Specializes in creating vector art and mockups. You can generate a design and then instantly see how it looks on a t-shirt, mug, or phone case.

Packify.ai: A niche wrapper focused on generating packaging designs and product photography for e-commerce.

These wrappers are fantastic for beginners, quick projects, or specialized tasks. They handle all the complex technical work behind the scenes, letting you focus purely on the creative act of prompting.

The Universal Language of Creation: Mastering the Art of Prompting

No matter which studio you enter, the language you use to communicate your vision is the prompt. A well-crafted prompt is like a detailed blueprint for your AI artist. The universal structure for a great prompt includes several key components:

Subject: The main focus of the image (e.g., "a wise old owl").

Action/Pose: What the subject is doing (e.g., "reading a book by candlelight").

Setting: The environment or background (e.g., "in a cozy, cluttered library").

Lighting: The mood and time of day (e.g., "warm, flickering candlelight").

Mood/Atmosphere: The overall feeling (e.g., "mysterious and scholarly").

Style: The artistic medium or influence (e.g., "in the style of a classic oil painting").

Technical Details: Camera angles, lens types, or composition (e.g., "close-up shot, shallow depth of field").

A prompt combining these elements would be: *"A wise old owl reading a book by candlelight in a cozy, cluttered library. The scene is lit by warm, flickering candlelight, creating a mysterious and scholarly mood. In the style of a classic oil painting, close-up shot, shallow depth of field."*

Advanced Techniques: Becoming a Digital Maestro

Once you've mastered the basics, you can begin to explore the advanced techniques that separate the amateur from the maestro.

Creating Consistent Characters: The Actor in Your AI Film

One of the biggest challenges in AI art has been creating the same character across multiple images. How do you ensure your hero looks the same from one scene to the next? By 2025, several powerful methods have emerged.

Method 1: Reference and Reinforcement (The Director's Method) This is the most common and accessible method. You start by generating an image of your character that you love. Then, you use that image as a **reference** for all future generations.

In **Midjourney V7**, you use the `--oref` (Omni Reference) parameter, followed by the URL of your character's image. This tells the AI to base the new character on the one in the reference image.

In platforms like **Leonardo AI**, there is a dedicated "Character Reference" feature where you can upload your image.

The key is to combine the reference image with a strong text prompt that **reinforces** the character's key features. For example: `--oref a young woman with fiery red hair and green eyes, wearing her signature leather jacket, standing in a rainy cyberpunk alley.` This combination of visual reference and textual reinforcement is crucial for consistency.

Method 2: Training a Custom Model with LoRA (The Method Actor) For ultimate consistency, you can train a small, specialized AI model of your character. This is done using a technique called **LoRA (Low-Rank Adaptation)**. Think of a LoRA as a small "patch" or "fine-tuning" file that you apply to a large base model like Stable Diffusion. You train the LoRA on 15-30 images of your character, and it learns their specific features. Once trained, you can activate the LoRA and use a special "trigger word" in your prompt to summon your character with incredible accuracy. This method requires more effort upfront but provides the highest level of consistency, making it perfect for comic books or animated series.

The Power User's Canvas: A Gentle Introduction to ComfyUI

For those who crave ultimate control, there is **ComfyUI**. Imagine instead of just writing a prompt, you could build the entire image generation process yourself, like a flowchart or a set of Lego blocks. That is ComfyUI. It is a node-based interface for open-source models like Stable Diffusion and Flux.

In ComfyUI, your workflow is a visual map:

Nodes are the blocks that perform actions (e.g., `Load Checkpoint` to load the main AI model, `CLIP Text Encode` to process your prompt, `KSampler` to generate the image).

Edges are the wires that connect these nodes, showing how data flows from one step to the next.

While it looks complex, a basic workflow is simple: you load a model, write a prompt, and generate an image. The real power comes from adding more nodes. For example, to use a LoRA model you've trained, you simply add a `Load LoRA` node into your workflow, chaining it between your main model and the sampler.

ComfyUI has a steeper learning curve, but it offers unparalleled control over every aspect of image generation. Best of all, entire workflows can be saved and shared simply by dragging and dropping the final PNG image, which contains all the necessary data in its metadata.

The world of AI image creation is a vast and wondrous garden, filled with powerful tools and endless possibilities. By understanding the different artists in this digital atelier, mastering the universal language of prompting, and daring to experiment with advanced techniques, you can cultivate your imagination and bring any vision, no matter how fantastical, to vibrant life.

Unveiling the Canvas: Understanding AI Image Creation and Mastering the Art of Prompting

The Alchemy of Pixels: Understanding How AI Image Creation Works

Imagine a vast, digital atelier where millions of images have been deconstructed, analyzed, and reassembled countless times. This is the foundation of AI image creation - a process that's part science, part magic, and entirely revolutionary.

At its core, AI image generation relies on deep learning models, specifically a type called Generative Adversarial Networks (GANs) or more recently, diffusion models. These are like two artists working in tandem: one creating, the other critiquing, constantly pushing each other to improve.

The process begins with training. The AI is shown millions of images, each labeled with descriptive text. It learns to associate certain visual elements with specific words or phrases. It's as if the AI is building a vast mental catalog, understanding that "furry" often goes with certain textures, or "sunset" with particular color palettes.

When you input a prompt, the AI doesn't simply piece together existing images. Instead, it creates something new from scratch, pixel by pixel. It starts with random noise - imagine a TV screen showing static - and gradually refines this into a coherent image that matches your description.

This refinement process is where the magic happens. The AI uses what it's learned about the relationships between words and visual elements to guide its creation. It's like an artist with an infinite palette, mixing and matching elements to best represent your prompt.

The level of detail in this process is staggering. The AI considers aspects like composition, lighting, texture, and style, all inferred from your prompt and its training. It might generate hundreds of variations internally before settling on the final output.

Recent advancements, particularly in diffusion models, have dramatically improved the quality and coherence of generated images. These models work by gradually removing noise from the image, a process that allows for more fine-grained control and often results in more photorealistic outputs.

One of the most fascinating aspects of this technology is its ability to understand and combine concepts. When you ask for a "steampunk cat," the AI doesn't just overlay gears on a cat picture. It understands the aesthetic of steampunk and the characteristics of cats, blending them into something new and coherent.

However, it's important to remember that AI image generation has limitations. The AI can only create based on what it's been trained on, and its understanding is fundamentally different from human comprehension. It doesn't truly "understand" concepts as we do, but rather has learned complex patterns of association.

This is why prompting is so crucial. The way you phrase your request can significantly impact the output. You're not just describing an image; you're guiding the AI through its vast catalog of learned associations, helping it piece together the vision in your mind.

As we continue to refine these models and techniques, the line between human and AI creativity becomes increasingly blurred. We're not just creating tools for image generation; we're developing new ways of visualizing ideas and concepts. It's a collaboration between human imagination and computational power that's redefining the boundaries of visual art and design.

Da Sachin Sharma

Da Sachin Sharma

The Language of Creation: Understanding Prompting for Image Generation

Prompting an AI to generate an image is like conducting an orchestra with words. Your prompt is the score, each word a note that guides the AI in composing a visual symphony. Mastering this language of creation is key to unlocking the full potential of AI image generation. Let's explore the nuances of this art form.

Text to Image: Painting with Words

Text-to-image prompting is the most common form of AI image generation. Here, your words are the brushstrokes that bring your vision to life. The key is to be both specific and evocative. Consider this process:

1. Start with the core concept: "A majestic lion"

2. Add context: "standing on a cliff"

3. Set the mood: "at sunset"

4. Specify style: "in the style of watercolor painting"

Your final prompt might be: "A majestic lion standing on a cliff at sunset, in the style of watercolor painting."

Tips for effective text-to-image prompting:

- Be specific about details, but leave room for the AI's interpretation.

- Use descriptive adjectives to convey mood and atmosphere.

- Experiment with artistic styles and techniques in your prompts.

- Consider the composition: foreground, background, perspective.

Remember, the AI doesn't understand images as we do. It's interpreting your words based on its training. The more guidance you provide, the closer the result will be to your vision.

Image to Image: Guided Transformation

Image-to-image prompting is like giving the AI a starting point and directions for a journey. You provide an initial image and instructions on how to modify or expand it. This can be used for:

- Style transfer: "Transform this photograph into a Van Gogh painting"

- Content editing: "Replace the car in this image with a horse-drawn carriage"

- Expansion: "Extend this landscape to show what's beyond the frame"

When using image-to-image prompting, be clear about what elements of the original image you want to preserve and what you want to change. Your prompt might look like:

"Using this cityscape as a base, transform it into a futuristic metropolis with flying cars and neon signs, maintaining the original composition."

Prompt Structure: Architecting Your Vision

The structure of your prompt can significantly influence the output. A well-structured prompt is like a well-designed blueprint. Here's a general structure you can follow:

1. Subject: What's the main focus of the image?

2. Action/Pose: What is the subject doing?

3. Setting: Where is the scene taking place?

4. Lighting: Describe the lighting conditions.

5. Mood/Atmosphere: What's the overall feeling?

6. Style: Specify any particular artistic style or technique.

7. Technical Details: Mention camera angles, shot types, etc., if relevant.

For example:

"A curious red fox (subject) peeking out (action) from a snow-covered pine forest (setting) under the Northern Lights (lighting). The scene should evoke a sense of wonder and mystery (mood) and be

rendered in a style reminiscent of Studio Ghibli animations (style) with a low-angle shot (technical detail)."

Negative Prompts: Sculpting by Subtraction

Negative prompts are like telling the AI what not to include. They're particularly useful for refining your image and avoiding unwanted elements. For example:

Positive prompt: "A serene beach at sunset with palm trees"

Negative prompt: "No people, no buildings, no boats"

This tells the AI to focus on the natural elements of the beach scene without human presence or structures.

Tips for using negative prompts:

- Use them to avoid common AI quirks (e.g., "no extra fingers" for human figures)

- Exclude elements that might detract from your main subject

- Refine style elements (e.g., "no oversaturation" or "no cartoon style")

Advanced Techniques: Fine-tuning Your Artistic Voice

As you become more comfortable with basic prompting, you can explore advanced techniques:

1. Weighting: Some AI models allow you to assign importance to different parts of your prompt. For example: "A mystical forest (1.5) | glowing mushrooms (1.2) | fairies (0.8)"

2. Prompting for Composition: Use terms like "rule of thirds," "golden ratio," or "symmetrical composition" to guide the image structure.

3. Temporal Prompts: For models that support it, you can create prompts that suggest motion or time passage, like "A flower blooming in timelapse"

4. Hybrid Techniques: Combine text-to-image and image-to-image. Generate an initial image with text, then refine it using image-to-image prompts.

5. Style Mixing: Experiment with combining different artistic styles, like "A cityscape in a style that blends Art Deco with Cyberpunk"

Remember, prompting is an art form in itself. It requires practice, experimentation, and a willingness to iterate. Each AI model has its quirks and strengths, so what works well in one might need adjustment in another.

As you explore the world of AI image generation, think of yourself as both an artist and a translator. You're not just describing an image; you're learning to speak the language of visual creation in a way that AI can understand and execute. With time and practice, you'll develop an intuitive sense for crafting prompts that consistently produce stunning, imaginative results.

The beauty of this process is that it combines the boundless creativity of the human mind with the vast capabilities of AI. In this collaboration, we're not just generating images; we're exploring new frontiers of visual expression, limited only by our imagination and our ability to guide these digital artists with our words.

Applying Thinking Styles to Image Prompting

Remember our journey through the garden of thinking styles? Those same approaches - literal, lateral, and technical - can be powerful tools in crafting image prompts. Let's explore how to apply these thinking styles to create rich, diverse, and effective prompts for AI image generation.

Literal Thinking: The Foundation

Literal thinking in image prompting is about being clear, specific, and straightforward. It's the bedrock upon which we build our visual creations.

Example:

"A red apple sitting on a wooden table with a white background."

This prompt is clear and unambiguous. The AI knows exactly what elements to include and how to arrange them. Literal thinking is especially useful when you have a precise image in mind and want the AI to recreate it as accurately as possible.

Lateral Thinking: The Imagination Catalyst

Lateral thinking allows us to make unexpected connections and create unique, often surreal images. It's about combining concepts in novel ways.

Example:

"A library where the books are clouds and the librarians are wind spirits."

This prompt uses lateral thinking to create a whimsical and unexpected scene. It combines the familiar concept of a library with fantastical elements, encouraging the AI to create something truly unique.

Technical Thinking: The Detail Refiner

Technical thinking in image prompting involves understanding and specifying the more technical aspects of image creation, such as composition, lighting, and style.

Example:

"A close-up portrait of an elderly man, using Rembrandt lighting, with a shallow depth of field. Shot on a full-frame sensor at f/2.8, ISO 400, 1/125 sec shutter speed."

This prompt demonstrates technical knowledge of photography and art, giving the AI very specific parameters to work with. It's likely to result in a highly detailed and professional-looking image.

Combining Thinking Styles: The Masterpiece Maker

The real magic happens when we combine these thinking styles. Let's look at an example that incorporates all three:

"Create a hyper-realistic (technical) underwater scene of a futuristic city (lateral) where jellyfish-shaped buildings float amidst schools of robotic fish (lateral). The image should be composed using the rule of thirds (technical), with a large, bioluminescent jellyfish-skyscraper as the main focal point in the foreground (literal). Use a cool color palette dominated by blues and greens (technical), with pops of neon pink and purple from the city's lights (literal). The lighting should simulate light filtering through water, creating caustic patterns on the structures (technical)."

This prompt combines:

- Literal thinking in its specific descriptions of elements and colors

- Lateral thinking in its imaginative concept of an underwater futuristic city with jellyfish buildings

- Technical thinking in its use of compositional rules, lighting techniques, and color theory

By blending these thinking styles, we create a prompt that is simultaneously precise, imaginative, and technically informed. This gives the AI a rich set of instructions to work with, increasing the likelihood of a stunning and unique output.

Tips for Combining Thinking Styles in Image Prompts

1. Start with a Lateral Concept: Begin with an imaginative idea that combines unexpected elements.

2. Refine with Literal Details: Add specific, concrete details to ground your imaginative concept and make it more vivid.

3. Enhance with Technical Specifications: Incorporate technical elements like composition, lighting, and style to give your image a professional quality.

4. Balance is Key: Ensure that your prompt isn't overwhelmed by any one thinking style. A good prompt often has elements of all three.

5. Iterate and Experiment: Don't be afraid to generate multiple images, tweaking your prompt each time to see how different combinations of thinking styles affect the output.

Remember, the goal is not just to create an image, but to effectively translate your vision into a language the AI can understand and execute. By consciously applying these different thinking styles, you're not just prompting an AI - you're engaging in a new form of artistic expression, where your ability to imagine and articulate becomes as important as any traditional artistic skill.

As you practice combining these thinking styles in your prompts, you'll develop a unique "voice" in AI image generation. You'll learn which combinations work best for different types of images, and how to quickly switch between thinking styles to achieve your desired results.

In essence, you're not just learning to create images - you're learning to think in images, to see the world through the lens of possibility that AI image generation offers. And in doing so, you're pushing the boundaries of what's possible in visual creation, one prompt at a time.

Moving Pictures: The Art and Science of AI Video Creation

Welcome to the grand cinema of artificial intelligence. Just a year ago, this was a small, experimental art house theater, playing short, often glitchy, silent films that were fascinating novelties. Today, in 2025, it has exploded into a sprawling, state-of-the-art multiplex. The screens are brighter, the films are longer and more coherent, and for the first time, they have a voice. The magic lantern of the digital age is no longer just projecting simple animations; it is learning to tell stories, direct actors, and compose symphonies of sight and sound.

This chapter is your all-access pass to this new world of AI filmmaking. We will start in the projection booth, understanding the science behind how these digital dreams are made, from **Text-to-Video** to **Image-to-Video** and **Video-to-Video** transformations. We'll then step onto the set to learn the language of cinematography, mastering **camera shots and angles** to direct our AI crew. We'll sit in the writer's room, learning how to create a **storyboard** with prompts and control the narrative with the **First Frame/Last Frame** concept.

Finally, we'll tour the major production studios of 2025. We'll visit the blockbuster sets of **Google's Veo 3** and **Midjourney Video**, explore the dynamic stages of **Runway** and **Luma's Dream Machine**, and discover the groundbreaking work of international players like **Kling**, **Seedance**, and **Minimax**. We will learn their unique prompting styles, how to create **consistent characters**, and explore their revolutionary new capabilities in **sound and lip-syncing**.

Grab your director's chair. It's time to make movie magic.

The Science of Moving Pixels: How AI Video is Made

At its heart, AI video creation is an extension of the image generation magic we explored earlier, but with the added complexity of time and motion. The AI models are trained not just on images, but on vast libraries of video clips, learning the physics of movement, the rhythm of action, and the language of cinema.

There are three primary ways we can direct our AI filmmaker:

Text-to-Video: This is the purest form of creation, where you act as the screenwriter, describing a scene entirely with words. The AI interprets your prompt and generates a brand-new video from digital noise, choreographing every element from the ground up.

Image-to-Video: Here, you act as a director with a photograph. You provide a starting image and then give the AI instructions on how to bring it to life. The AI animates the still image, adding motion to characters, environments, and the camera itself.

Video-to-Video: This is like being a visual effects supervisor. You provide an existing video clip and instruct the AI to transform it. This could mean changing the style (turning a live-action clip into an anime sequence), replacing objects, or altering the background, all while preserving the original motion.

The biggest challenge for all these methods is **temporal consistency**—ensuring a character or object looks the same from one moment to the next. The models of 2025 have made huge leaps in this area, making coherent, story-driven videos a reality.

The Director's Toolkit: Understanding Camera and Shots

To prompt like a director, you must first learn to think like one. Understanding the language of cinematography is the key to crafting technical prompts that give you precise control over your final video.

Shot Types (The Framing):

Wide Shot (or Long Shot): Shows the entire subject from head to toe and their surrounding environment. Use this to establish a scene or show a character's relationship to their location.

Medium Shot: Shows the subject from the waist up. This is great for capturing body language and interactions between characters.

Close-Up: Fills the screen with the subject's face. Use this to convey emotion and intimacy.

Extreme Close-Up: Focuses on a single detail, like a character's eyes or a ticking watch, to create tension or highlight significance.

Camera Angles (The Perspective):

Eye-Level Shot: The most neutral angle, where the camera is at the subject's eye level.

Low-Angle Shot: The camera looks up at the subject, making them appear powerful, heroic, or intimidating.

High-Angle Shot: The camera looks down on the subject, which can make them seem vulnerable, small, or insignificant.

Bird's-Eye View (or Top-Down Shot): The camera is directly overhead, offering a god-like perspective of the scene.

Camera Movements (The Motion):

Pan: The camera swivels horizontally from a fixed point (like turning your head left or right).

Tilt: The camera swivels vertically from a fixed point (like nodding your head up or down).

Dolly (or Tracking Shot): The entire camera moves forward, backward, or alongside the subject. A "dolly in" moves closer, creating intimacy or tension. A "dolly out" moves away, revealing more of the scene.

Zoom: The lens adjusts to make the subject appear closer or farther away without the camera physically moving. A "zoom in" can feel more aggressive than a dolly in.

By including these terms in your prompts (e.g., *"Low-angle tracking shot of a hero running through a futuristic city"*), you give the AI a clear and technical blueprint for how to film your scene.

The Blueprint: Storyboarding and Controlling the Narrative

For any video longer than a few seconds, trying to describe everything in a single prompt is a recipe for chaos. The professional approach is to **storyboard with prompts**. You break your story into a sequence of individual shots and write a specific prompt for each one.

Example Storyboard: A 15-second ad for a new coffee brand, "Aura Brew."

Shot 1 (0-5 seconds):

Prompt: *Extreme close-up shot, slow motion. Dark, aromatic coffee beans cascade onto a clean, white surface. Soft, warm studio lighting.*

Shot 2 (5-10 seconds):

Prompt: *Medium shot. A person's hands pour steaming hot water over coffee grounds in a pour-over brewer. Steam rises gracefully. The scene is cozy and inviting.*

Shot 3 (10-15 seconds):

Prompt: *Close-up shot. A woman with a serene expression takes the first sip from a ceramic mug of Aura Brew. A gentle smile forms on her face. Sunlight streams through a nearby window.*

The First and Last Frame: Mastering Loops and Transitions

A powerful technique offered by advanced models like Midjourney and Luma is the ability to control the **first and last frame** of your video. This gives you incredible control over your narrative flow.

Creating Seamless Loops: By making the first and last frames identical, you can create perfect, endlessly looping videos (GIFs). This is ideal for animated backgrounds, social media avatars, or mesmerizing artistic clips.

Controlling Transitions: You can use this feature to ensure a smooth transition between two different AI-generated clips. By making the last frame of your first video the same as the first frame of your second video, you can stitch them together seamlessly, creating a longer, more cohesive narrative.

The Grand Studios: A Tour of the 2025 Video Platforms

The 2025 AI video landscape is dominated by several major studios, each with its own technology, artistic style, and prompting language.

Google Veo 3: The Hollywood Studio with a Voice

Google's Veo 3, launched globally in mid-2025, is a titan of the industry. Integrated into Google's ecosystem, it's a powerful, high-fidelity model that has set a new standard for realism and, most importantly, **sound**.

Capabilities: Veo 3 excels at creating stunningly realistic, 4K video clips with accurate physics. Its killer feature is

native audio generation. It can create background music, sound effects, and even **lip-synced dialogue** directly from your prompt, a capability its competitors are still racing to match. It understands nuanced cinematic language ("timelapse," "aerial shot") and can generate clips up to 8 seconds long.

Prompt Formula: of...

Sample Prompt: *"Medium shot of a woman sitting at a cafe table, cinematic style. She looks at the camera and says, 'I think this is the beginning of a beautiful* *friendship.' The sound of city ambiance and soft jazz music in the background."*

Midjourney Video: The Auteur's Art House

After conquering the world of AI images, Midjourney officially entered the video arena in June 2025 with its "Model V1". True to its roots, Midjourney Video is the choice for the creator who prioritizes aesthetic quality and artistic control above all else.

Capabilities: It produces visually stunning, coherent videos with the same artistic flair as its image counterpart. It can generate up to **60 seconds of video** from a text prompt or, impressively, from just six reference images. It also includes a dedicated video upscaler and

start/end frame controls for creating seamless loops. Recent updates have also introduced

lip-sync capabilities, further enhancing its narrative potential.

Prompt Formula: ,,, `[Lighting], --ar [aspect ratio] --v 1`

Sample Prompt: *"A knight in shining armor riding a horse through a misty forest, cinematic, volumetric lighting, epic fantasy style --ar 16:9 --v 1"*

Kling: The Action Movie Specialist

Developed by Kuaishou, Kling has emerged as a powerhouse, particularly for generating dynamic, action-packed scenes with complex motion.

Capabilities: Kling can generate up to **two minutes of 1080p video** and has a remarkable understanding of physics, accurately simulating the movement of objects and characters. It excels at creating videos with significant and realistic motion and now supports

lip-sync for dialogue.

Prompt Formula: ,, [Motion Instructions]

Sample Prompt: *"A red sports car drifts around a sharp corner on a wet city street at night, cinematic style with high-contrast neon lighting and sharp focus, the camera tracks the car at a low angle with motion blur to emphasize speed."*

Runway Gen-4: The All-in-One Production Suite

Runway continues its reign as the Swiss Army knife of AI video, evolving into a comprehensive production suite with its Gen-4 model. It offers a vast array of tools for creators who want to be hands-on with every step of the process.

Capabilities: Runway's biggest advantage is its suite of tools. **Consistent Characters** can be achieved by providing a reference image.

Layout Sketch lets you draw a composition to guide the AI, and **Act-One** allows for expressive character animation using a driving video. It also supports

4K upscaling and has its own **lip-sync** tool.

Prompt Formula (Chat Mode): Start with a simple prompt and refine it through conversation.

Sample Prompt (Iterative):

Initial Prompt: *"A mechanical bull runs across a desert."*

Refinement 1: *"Make the desert dusty, and have the dust trail behind the bull as it moves."*

Refinement 2: *"Now, add a handheld camera tracking shot that follows the bull."*

Luma Labs' Dream Machine: The Dream Weaver

Luma AI's Dream Machine, powered by their new Ray2 model, is designed to create fluid, cinematic, and often surreal videos with incredible ease.

Capabilities: Dream Machine excels at creating lifelike motion and high-quality visuals from simple text prompts or images. Its **Modify Video** tool is a powerful video-to-video feature that allows you to transform existing footage while keeping the original motion intact. It also supports

start/end frame control for perfect loops.

Prompt Formula: , [Action],,, [Camera Instructions]

Sample Prompt: *"A glass apple shattering in slow-motion, the shards catching the sunlight as they fly through the air, hyper-realistic, cinematic, close-up shot."*

Rising Stars: Seedance & Minimax

Seedance: Developed by ByteDance, Seedance has shocked the community by topping benchmarks for its incredible **multi-shot understanding**. Unlike models that create one continuous clip, Seedance can interpret prompts that describe a sequence of different shots (e.g., "Wide shot of a castle, then a close-up of the queen's face"), making it a true narrative tool.

Prompt Formula: . Then, . Then, .

Sample Prompt: *"A wide shot of a futuristic city at night. Then, a close-up of a flying car speeding through a neon canyon. Finally, an extreme close-up of the driver's determined face."*

Minimax: This model, often found integrated into other apps, excels at creating short, high-quality clips perfect for social media B-roll or overlays. It has a particular talent for creating charming **Ghibli-style animations** and supports both text-to-video and image-to-video.

Prompt Formula (Image-to-Video): is now [Action].

Sample Prompt (with an image of a girl): *"The girl is now waving happily at the camera."*

The world of AI video is no longer a distant dream. It is a tangible, accessible, and powerful new medium for creative expression. By understanding the language of film and the unique dialects of each AI platform, you can move beyond being a mere spectator. You can become the director, the choreographer, and the storyteller of digital dreams.

The Googleplex Studio: Directing with Veo 3

In the bustling metropolis of AI video creation, a new skyscraper has risen, casting a long shadow over the landscape. This is the Googleplex Studio, home to **Veo 3**, a titan of the industry that has redefined what is possible in AI filmmaking. Unveiled at Google I/O 2025 and now available globally, Veo 3 is not just another tool; it is a full-fledged production house, a Hollywood-scale studio in your browser that, for the first time, has given our digital actors a voice.

This chapter is your exclusive set pass. We will step inside the Googleplex Studio and take the director's chair. You will learn how to command Veo 3 using the conversational language of a standard prompt, applying our core principles of Literal, Lateral, and Technical thinking to create stunning, photorealistic scenes. We will then move to the architect's office to master the precision of **JSON prompting**, a powerful technique for controlling every element of your production. We will explore how to breathe life into still images with **Image-to-Video** and, crucially, learn how to use the **Google Flow** ecosystem to create **consistent characters** across multiple shots, solving one of the greatest challenges in AI storytelling.

Welcome to the big leagues. It's time to direct your first blockbuster.

The Director's Chair: Standard Prompting with Veo 3

Veo 3's greatest strength is its profound understanding of natural and cinematic language. It is an AI that has been to film school. This allows us to direct it conversationally, blending our three core thinking styles into a single, powerful text prompt.

A great Veo 3 prompt is a symphony of instructions, telling the AI not just what to show, but what to hear and how to film it.

The Prompt Formula for Veo 3:

"""

Let's break down how our thinking styles apply:

Literal Thinking: This is your scene description. Be clear about the setting, the characters, and the core action. *"A woman sits at a cafe table."*

Lateral Thinking: This is your creative vision. What is the mood? What is the story? *"The scene is romantic and nostalgic, reminiscent of a classic film."*

Technical Thinking: This is your cinematic language. Use specific camera shots, angles, and sound cues. *"Medium shot," "soft jazz music in the background."*

Example in Action:

Let's create a short, emotionally resonant scene.

Prompt:

"Medium shot of a woman sitting at a cafe table in Paris, cinematic style. She looks directly at the camera with a gentle smile and says, 'I think this is the beginning of a beautiful friendship.' The sound of distant city ambiance and soft jazz music plays in the background."

Why This Works: This prompt gives Veo 3 a complete set of instructions. It knows the framing (Medium shot), the style (cinematic), the setting (Parisian cafe), the action (smiles at camera), the dialogue (which it will lip-sync), and the full audio landscape (ambiance and music). This multi-layered, conversational approach is the key to unlocking Veo 3's narrative power.

From Still to Story: Image-to-Video with Veo 3

Veo 3 is not just a text-to-video generator; it can also breathe life into a static image. This is a powerful tool for animators, artists, and storytellers who want to use a specific visual as the starting point for their scene.

The process is simple: you provide a starting image and then a text prompt that describes the motion you want to see.

The Image-to-Video Prompt Formula:

+ [Prompt describing the desired motion and sound]

Example in Action:

Imagine you have a beautiful AI-generated image of a majestic dragon sleeping on a mountain peak.

Prompt:

"The dragon slowly awakens. Its eye opens, glowing with inner fire. It lifts its head and lets out a deep, rumbling growl as smoke gently curls from its nostrils. The camera does a slow dolly zoom in on the dragon's eye."

This technique allows you to maintain perfect control over the initial art style and composition while leveraging

183

Veo 3's powerful animation and audio capabilities to bring your canvas to life.

The Production Workflow: Google Flow and Consistent Characters

One of the biggest hurdles in AI filmmaking has been creating consistent characters who look the same from one shot to the next. Google addresses this challenge by positioning Veo 3 within a larger production ecosystem called **Google Flow**. Think of Flow as your project management suite, a place to organize your scenes, control your camera, and, most importantly, manage your cast.

Within Flow, Veo 3 offers two key features for character consistency:

Jump To: This powerful tool allows you to take a character from one video and "jump" them into a completely new scene. You can generate a close-up of your hero in a cafe, and then use "Jump To" with a new prompt to place that same character in a wide shot walking through a park.

Extend: This feature is for continuing a scene. It takes the last frame of your video and generates the next sequence, ensuring the character's appearance and location remain perfectly consistent.

A Simple Workflow for a Two-Shot Scene:

Shot 1 - The Introduction: Generate your first clip in Flow.

Prompt: *"Close-up of a young woman with bright red hair and a leather jacket, standing on a rainy city street. She looks worried. She says, 'We have to go. Now.'"*

Shot 2 - The Action: Use the **"Jump To"** feature on the character of the woman.

Prompt: *"Wide shot. The same woman is now running down the crowded street, pushing past people. The camera tracks alongside her. The sound of sirens wails in the distance."*

By using the tools within the Google Flow ecosystem, you can finally move beyond creating isolated, beautiful clips and begin to craft true narrative sequences with a consistent cast of AI actors. While each clip is still limited to 8 seconds, these tools allow you to stitch together a longer, more coherent story, marking a monumental step forward for AI-powered filmmaking.

The Architect's Blueprint: Mastering JSON Prompting for AI Video

Throughout this book, we have learned to speak to our AI collaborators in the rich, flowing language of human conversation. We have acted as directors, guiding our digital actors with descriptive prose. But as the complexity of our visions grows, and as AI models become more sophisticated, there comes a time when a conversation is not enough. Sometimes, a director needs to hand their crew a precise, unambiguous, and perfectly structured blueprint.

Welcome to the world of **JSON prompting**.

If a standard text prompt is a conversation with your AI filmmaker, a JSON prompt is the architectural schematic. It is a method for providing instructions not as a narrative sentence, but as a structured data file. This may sound technical, but at its heart, it is the ultimate expression of control—a way to command every single element of your scene with the precision of an engineer. This chapter will demystify this powerful technique, showing you how to move from director to architect, with a special focus on unlocking the full cinematic potential of advanced models like **Google's Veo 3**.

From Conversation to Blueprint: What is JSON?

JSON, which stands for JavaScript Object Notation, is simply a way of organizing information in a clean, key-value format. Don't let the name intimidate you; the concept is incredibly simple.

Imagine you're writing down a recipe. A conversational approach might be: *"First, you take two cups of flour, then you add a teaspoon of salt and a tablespoon of sugar, and mix them together."*

A JSON approach would be like a perfectly organized recipe card:

JSON

```
{
  "step": 1,
  "action": "Mix Dry Ingredients",
  "ingredients":
}
```

That's it. JSON uses **keys** (like `"action"`) and **values** (like `"Mix Dry Ingredients"`) to structure information. This format is easy for both humans to read and, crucially, for computers to parse without any ambiguity.

Why Use a Blueprint for AI Video?

A single sentence is perfect for a simple shot. But what about a complex scene? Video is a multimodal medium— it has visuals, motion, characters, dialogue, and sound. Trying to cram all of those instructions into one paragraph can lead to ambiguity. The AI has to interpret your prose, and sometimes, its interpretation might not match your vision.

With JSON, we can control each of these elements independently. It allows us to provide a separate, detailed set of instructions for every single "department" in our virtual film studio—from cinematography and casting to sound design and special effects.

Directing Veo 3: The Ultimate JSON Use Case

Google's Veo 3 is the perfect candidate for JSON prompting because of its rich, multi-faceted capabilities. It doesn't just create silent video; it understands cinematic language, generates native audio, creates sound effects, and performs lip-sync for dialogue. Trying to control all these elements in a single sentence can become messy and ineffective. A JSON blueprint allows us to command each of Veo 3's features with absolute precision.

Let's take the same complex scene and write two prompts for it: one in the standard, conversational style and one as a structured JSON blueprint.

The Scene: A detective stands in a rainy, futuristic alley at night. He's lit by a neon sign and speaks a line of dialogue as a car speeds by in the background.

Method 1: The Standard Conversational Prompt

This is the method we've used throughout the book. It's powerful, intuitive, and great for most use cases.

Prompt: *"Medium shot of a detective in a trench coat standing in a rainy alley in a futuristic city at night. The scene is lit by the blue glow of a flickering neon sign that reads 'CYBERIA'. He looks tired and says, 'I've seen this all before.' As he speaks, a sleek, futuristic car speeds by in the background from right to left, splashing through a*

189

large puddle. The sound of heavy rain is constant, with a soft, melancholic synthesizer score and a sudden 'whoosh' as the car passes."

This is a very good prompt. It's descriptive and gives the AI a lot to work with. However, it relies on the AI to correctly interpret the relationship between all these elements.

Method 2: The JSON Architect's Blueprint

Now, let's build the exact same scene using a JSON prompt. Notice how every element gets its own clear, distinct instruction.

Prompt:

JSON

```json
{
    "scene_number": 1,
    "duration_seconds": 8,
    "setting": {
        "location": "A rain-slicked alley in a futuristic city at night.",
        "lighting": "Dominated by the cold, blue glow of a flickering neon sign that reads 'CYBERIA'.",
        "mood": "Noir, melancholic, tense."
    },
```

```
"camera": {

  "shot_type": "Medium Shot",

  "angle": "Eye-Level",

  "movement": "Static, with a slight
handheld feel."

  },

  "characters":,

  "background_action": {

  "description": "A sleek, futuristic
car without wheels speeds past from right
to left, splashing through a large puddle
on the ground."

  },

  "audio": {

  "background_music":    "A     soft,
melancholic synthesizer score, in the style
of Vangelis.",

  "sound_effects": [

    "Constant sound of heavy rain.",

    "A sudden 'whoosh' and splash as
the car passes by."

  ]

  }
```

}

Why This Blueprint Works

Unambiguous Control: Every element is explicitly defined. The AI doesn't have to guess what the lighting should be or what sound effects to add. It has a direct order for each "department."

Independent Elements: You can easily change one part without rewriting the whole prompt. Want to change the dialogue? Just edit the `"text"` value. Want a different camera angle? Change the `"angle"` value. This makes iteration and experimentation much faster.

Complex Scenes Made Simple: This structure makes it easy to manage scenes with multiple characters, actions, and audio cues. You could add another character object to the `"characters"` array, each with their own description and dialogue.

Consistency and Templates: This structure becomes a reusable template. For the next shot in your film, you can copy this JSON and simply change the values, ensuring a consistent style and format across your entire project.

JSON prompting represents the next step in our evolution as AI Orchestrators. It is the language we use when we want to move beyond suggestion and into precise, architectural command. While the art of the conversational prompt will always be a vital skill, learning to build a JSON blueprint empowers you to tackle more ambitious projects with a level of control that was, until now, the exclusive domain of a full production studio.

The Open-Source Studio: Crafting Videos with Community-Built Models

Beyond the polished walls of the major studios lies a vibrant, collaborative, and often chaotic world: the open-source video community. Think of this as a community workshop or a public-access film studio. Here, developers and artists from around the globe work with publicly released models like **Stable Video Diffusion** or experimental research models like Stanford's **W.A.L.T.**, building upon them to create new and exciting tools.

How to Access Open-Source Models

There are two main paths into this world, catering to different levels of technical comfort.

Wrapper Websites (The Easy Path): This is the most accessible route. Wrapper websites take powerful open-source models and "wrap" them in a simple, user-friendly interface. Platforms like **MimicPC** or **Replicate** host a wide variety of community-built video tools. You might find a tool specifically for creating the "AI Kissing" effect using the

Wan 2.1 model, or another for generating TikTok dances. These wrappers are like pre-packaged project kits—they make advanced, experimental effects easy to use without needing any technical setup.

ComfyUI (The Power User's Path): For those who crave ultimate control, there is **ComfyUI**. This is a node-based interface where you are the architect of your own video generation pipeline. Instead of a simple prompt box, you have a visual canvas where you connect different "nodes" (or blocks) to build a workflow.

A simple workflow might involve loading a model checkpoint (like Stable Video Diffusion), adding a text prompt, and connecting it to a sampler node to generate the video.

The real power lies in its modularity. You can chain multiple tools together. For example, you could build a workflow that first generates an image with a LoRA model, feeds that image into a video generation node to animate it, and then sends the resulting video to an upscaler node to enhance its quality.

The open-source world is more experimental and can have a steeper learning curve, but it offers unparalleled flexibility and a direct connection to the cutting edge of AI video development. It's where new trends are born and where you can truly build your own custom filmmaking tools.

The world of AI video is no longer a distant dream. It is a tangible, accessible, and powerful new medium for creative expression. By understanding the language of film and the unique dialects of each AI platform—from the grand commercial studios to the collaborative open-source workshops—you can move beyond being a mere spectator. You can become the director, the choreographer, and the storyteller of digital dreams.

The Future of Filmmaking: Node-Based Video Generation

As we look to the horizon, a new paradigm in AI filmmaking is emerging, one that moves beyond generating single clips to orchestrating entire films. This is the world of **node-based video generation**, and platforms like **LTX Studio** are leading the charge.

Imagine you are no longer just a director of individual shots, but the head of an entire AI-powered film studio. This is the promise of node-based generation. The process is a seamless flow from concept to final cut:

Script to Storyboard: You start by writing or pasting a script. The AI analyzes the text and automatically breaks it down into a sequence of scenes and shots, creating a visual storyboard for your entire film.

The Director's Canvas: This storyboard is presented on a node-based canvas. Each "node" represents a shot, a character, a camera angle, or a scene. You can see your entire film laid out visually.

Interactive Control: This is where the magic happens. You can interact with every node. Don't like the camera angle on Shot 3? Click the node and change it from a "medium shot" to a "close-up." Want to change a character's outfit in Scene 2? Edit the character node. You

197

can drag and drop shots to reorder them, adjust lighting, and control every aspect of the production.

One-Click Generation: Once you are happy with your visual blueprint, you generate the entire film. The AI takes your structured plan and creates all the video clips, stitches them together, adds sound, and delivers a complete movie.

This approach represents a monumental shift. It moves the user from being a prompter of isolated clips to a true **AI Director**, making high-level creative decisions while the AI handles the complex technical execution of every department—from cinematography and casting to editing and sound design. This is the future of storytelling, where anyone with a vision can command a virtual studio to bring their cinematic dreams to life.

The world of AI video is no longer a distant dream. It is a tangible, accessible, and powerful new medium for creative expression. By understanding the language of film and the unique dialects of each AI platform—from the grand commercial studios to the collaborative open-source workshops—you can move beyond being a mere spectator. You can become the director, the choreographer, and the storyteller of digital dreams.

Composing with Code: The Symphony of AI Music Creation

Imagine a world where melodies emerge not from instruments, but from algorithms; where harmonies are born in the binary realm of ones and zeros. This is the world of AI music creation—a fascinating intersection of art and technology that's redefining the boundaries of musical composition.

In 2025, this digital orchestra has matured. The simple, often repetitive tunes of early AI have given way to complex, emotionally resonant compositions complete with nuanced vocal performances. AI music generation is no longer just a novelty; it's a powerful creative partner. It's a virtual composer, producer, and session musician all rolled into one, capable of creating original pieces, accompanying existing melodies, or even mimicking the styles of famous artists.

This chapter is your conductor's baton. We will peek behind the curtain to understand how these AI musicians think. We will tour the grand concert halls of the leading AI music platforms, from the multifaceted maestro

SUNO to the collaborative composer **Udio**. Most importantly, you will learn the art of prompting—the universal language for conducting this digital orchestra—and master the advanced techniques needed to transform your lyrical ideas and musical concepts into fully-realized symphonies.

Behind the Curtain: How AI Music Generation Works

At its core, AI music generation is like teaching a computer to understand, interpret, and create music. The process begins with training data—vast datasets of MIDI files, audio recordings, and sheet music. The AI, often a neural network like a Transformer, learns to recognize patterns in melody, harmony, rhythm, and genre-specific characteristics.

When you provide a prompt, the AI uses Natural Language Processing (NLP) to interpret your words and translate them into musical parameters. It then uses a generative model to compose the music, making a series of predictions about what should come next based on what it has learned. Advanced systems can apply style transfer, incorporate rule-based systems to ensure musical coherence, and use audio synthesis to generate the final, polished audio output.

The Virtuosos of AI Music: A Tour of the 2025 Platforms

In the grand concert hall of AI music creation, certain tools stand out as true virtuosos, each with its own unique strengths and specialties.

SUNO: The Multifaceted Maestro

SUNO has firmly established itself as the comprehensive, all-in-one studio for AI music. It's a multifaceted tool capable of generating complete songs—including surprisingly realistic vocals—from simple text prompts. The platform has evolved significantly, with its

v4.5 update in mid-2025 introducing a suite of professional-grade features that give creators unparalleled control.

Key Capabilities: SUNO excels at generating full tracks up to eight minutes long. Its vocal synthesis is a standout feature, capable of producing everything from delicate, intimate performances to powerful deliveries. The most significant 2025 update, however, is the introduction of **Stem Separation**. This game-changing feature allows a finished song to be split into up to 12 clean tracks (e.g., separate files for vocals, drums, bass, guitar), which can then be exported into a traditional

Digital Audio Workstation (DAW) like Ableton Live or Logic Pro for detailed mixing and mastering.

Udio: The Collaborative Composer

Udio has emerged as a powerful and user-friendly alternative, focusing on a seamless and intuitive creation process. It's like a collaborative partner, ready to turn your ideas into polished tracks with remarkable ease.

Key Capabilities: Udio offers a powerful suite of features, including text-to-song and lyrics-to-song generation, music extension capabilities to seamlessly lengthen tracks, and a voice remover to create instrumental versions. A key feature is its

Style Reference tool, which allows Pro subscribers to generate new music based on the vibe of a reference audio track. While it doesn't yet have stem separation, its high-quality output and generous free plan make it incredibly accessible.

The Specialist's Toolkit: Other Notable Instruments

Beyond the two giants, a rich ecosystem of specialized tools has emerged, each focusing on a specific part of the music creation process.

For Background Music: Platforms like **Soundraw** and **Beatoven** excel at creating high-quality, royalty-free background music for videos and podcasts.

For Songwriters: Riffusion is a fantastic free tool for turning lyrics into simple song ideas, while **Amadeus Code** acts as an AI songwriting assistant, suggesting melodies and chord progressions.

For Producers: A suite of AI-powered plugins from companies like **Unison Audio** can generate specific elements like basslines (**Bass Dragon**), chord progressions (**Chord Genie**), or drum patterns (**Drum Monkey**), integrating directly into a producer's existing workflow.

The Conductor's Guide: Mastering AI-Assisted Music Creation

To conduct this digital orchestra effectively, you need to speak its language. Mastering the art of the prompt is the key to transforming your musical vision into a sonic reality.

The Architectural Blueprint: Understanding Song Structure

Before you write a single lyric or prompt, you must think like an architect. A song is a structure, an emotional journey with a beginning, a middle, and an end. In my experience creating over 15,000 songs, I've learned that the most common reason a track fails is a weak or non-existent structure. The AI is a brilliant performer, but it needs a solid blueprint to build upon.

Let's break down the essential components of that blueprint:

The Intro: This is the front door to your song. Its only job is to grab the listener's attention and set the mood. It can be a simple instrumental hook, a spoken word phrase, or an atmospheric soundscape.

The Verse: This is the storyteller. The verses are where you build your narrative, introduce characters, and describe scenes. Musically, verses are often less intense than the chorus, creating a sense of progression and building anticipation.

The Pre-Chorus: This is the ramp-up. It's a short section that builds a bridge of tension between the verse and the chorus. It signals to the listener that something big is about to happen.

The Chorus: This is the heart of your song. It's the most memorable, catchy, and emotionally potent section. The chorus should contain your core message or theme, and it's the part you want listeners to be singing in their heads long after the song is over.

The Post-Chorus (or Hook): This is the earworm. Immediately following the chorus, this is often a simple, repetitive musical or lyrical phrase that reinforces the song's main idea and makes it even more unforgettable.

The Bridge: This is the detour. The bridge offers a change of pace, a shift in perspective, or a new musical idea. It breaks up the repetition of the verse-chorus cycle and provides a moment of reflection before launching into the final, powerful chorus.

The Solo: This is the instrumental spotlight. Often taking the place of a bridge or a third verse, a solo allows a specific instrument (like a guitar or saxophone) to take center stage and express the song's emotion without words.

The Outro: This is the farewell. It can be a fade-out of the chorus, a final instrumental flourish, or a quiet, reflective conclusion that leaves the listener with a lasting impression.

My Creative Process: From Feeling to Final Track

Every song I create starts with a feeling. It might be an emotion, a specific beat I have in my head, or a genre I want to explore. Sometimes, the initial spark is a melody. I'll often hum a tune into my phone, record a simple acapella, and then use SUNO's **Audio Upload** feature to build an entire song around that single melodic idea. This method has been a revelation for me, allowing me to turn all the poems I've ever written into fully realized songs, each with its own unique sonic identity.

By understanding the architectural components above, I can take that initial feeling and give it a structure. I decide where the story will unfold (the verses), what the central, repeatable message will be (the chorus), and how I'll create moments of tension and release (the bridge and solos). This structure is the map that guides both my creativity and the AI's generation process.

The Universal Language of Music Prompting

Regardless of the platform you use, a great music prompt is built on a foundation of clear musical intent. The more specific you are, the better the result will be.

Core Prompt Components:

Genre and Style: This is the most crucial element. It sets the entire framework. Instead of "rock," be specific:

"90s grunge rock anthem," "70s psychedelic rock," or "modern indie rock."

Mood and Theme: Describe the feeling you want to evoke. Use evocative adjectives like "melancholy," "uplifting," "aggressive," "dreamy," or "nostalgic."

Instrumentation: List the key instruments you want to hear. This shapes the texture of the song. For example: "acoustic guitar, upright bass, gentle piano, and a string quartet."

Tempo and Rhythm: Specify the speed and feel. You can use BPM (e.g., "120 BPM") or descriptive terms like "slow ballad," "up-tempo dance beat," or "mid-tempo shuffle."

Vocal Style: Describe the voice you imagine. "A raspy male voice," "breathy female vocals," "a powerful gospel choir," or "harmonizing backup vocals."

Advanced Prompting Techniques

Once you've mastered the basics, you can use these advanced techniques to gain even more control.

Using Lyrical Cues for Structure: The most powerful way to control a song's structure is through the lyrics themselves. Use bracketed tags like [Verse], [Chorus], , , or [Intro] to explicitly define the different sections of your song. The AI will recognize these tags and build the music accordingly.

Genre Blending: Don't be afraid to create unique fusion styles. Prompts like "A blend of country and trap music" or "classical orchestral music with electronic glitch elements" can lead to incredibly original results.

Using Sensory Language: Go beyond simple descriptions. Use sensory language to describe the production style. For example, instead of "reverb on vocals," try "glistening, cavernous reverb on ethereal female vocals." Instead of "distorted bass," try "a gritty, overdriven bassline that rattles the chest."

Iterative Refinement: Your first generation is rarely the final one. Use it as a starting point. Listen to what the AI created and refine your prompt. If the drums are too simple, add "complex, syncopated drum pattern" to your next prompt. This back-and-forth process is key to honing in on your perfect sound.

Mastering SUNO: Your AI Production Studio

SUNO has evolved from a simple music generator into a comprehensive production environment. To master it, you need to understand its full suite of tools, from initial creation to final polish.

The Two Creative Paths: Simple vs. Custom Mode

SUNO offers two primary ways to create, catering to different needs.

Simple Mode: This is the fastest way to get started. You simply write a description of the song you want (e.g., "A happy pop song about a vacation with fast piano music"), and SUNO generates both the lyrics and the music. It's perfect for quick brainstorming or for users who don't have specific lyrics in mind.

Custom Mode: This mode gives you granular control. Here, you can input your own lyrics, specify the style of music, and decide whether you want an instrumental track. This is the path for creators who have a clear lyrical or structural idea they want to bring to life.

Crafting Lyrics: The Heart of Your Song

In Custom Mode, you have several options for lyrics.

Write Your Own: Paste your pre-written lyrics directly into the lyrics box.

AI-Assisted Writing: Use SUNO's built-in lyric generator, powered by the ReMi model, to get started. You can describe a theme, and it will generate tailored lines for you. For more complex narratives, you can also use an external LLM like ChatGPT or Claude to write lyrics and then paste them into SUNO.

Creating Instrumentals: If you don't want vocals, simply toggle the "Instrumental" switch in Custom Mode. SUNO will then compose a track based solely on your style prompt, ignoring the lyrics box.

The Producer's Toolkit: Upload, Remix, and Edit

This is where SUNO's 2025 updates truly shine, transforming it into a powerful editing and production tool.

Audio Upload: Have a melody you hummed into your phone or a cool drum loop you created? The **Upload Audio** feature lets you import your own sound clips (up to 8 minutes for Pro users) as a starting point. SUNO will then analyze your audio and generate music that complements or builds upon it, effectively turning your raw ideas into fully orchestrated pieces.

Remix and Remaster:

Remix: This feature allows you to take any song on the SUNO platform (if permissions are enabled) and create your own version. You can change the lyrics, alter the style, or adjust the speed to make it your own.

Remaster: This tool is designed to improve the audio quality of older songs (e.g., those made with v3.5) by regenerating them using the newer v4 model. While it can enhance clarity, be aware that it's a full regeneration, not just a filter, so it can sometimes alter the original feel or emotion of the track.

The Advanced Song Editor: The June 2025 update introduced a professional-grade editor that gives you surgical control over your creations.

Waveform Editing: You can now see the visual waveform of your track, making it easy to identify specific sections to edit.

Replace Section: This is the most powerful editing tool. Instead of regenerating an entire song to fix one bad line, you can now highlight just that section—a single word, a guitar riff, a drum fill—and regenerate only that part, leaving the rest of your song intact.

Creative Sliders: Fine-tune the vibe of your track with sliders for "weirdness," "style strength," and "audio strength." This allows you to experiment with unconventional harmonies or create interesting genre fusions.

Stem Separation (The Pro Move): For ultimate creative control, SUNO's **Stem Separation** feature is a game-changer. It allows you to export your finished song as up to 12 individual audio tracks (stems)—isolating the vocals, drums, bass, guitar, and other instruments. You can then import these stems into a professional Digital

Audio Workstation (DAW) like Logic Pro, Ableton Live, or Pro Tools for detailed mixing, mastering, and adding your own live instruments. This feature bridges the gap between AI ideation and human-led professional production, making SUNO an invaluable tool in a modern musician's workflow.

The symphony of AI music is just beginning its performance. By learning to conduct these powerful new instruments with skill and creativity, you can compose music that was once impossible, transforming the ideas in your head into fully orchestrated realities.

Sculpting in the Void: The Dawn of AI 3D Generation

For years, we have learned to paint with pixels and direct moving pictures, working on the flat canvas of a screen. But in 2025, the AI art studio has thrown open a new door, inviting us to step off the canvas and into the workshop. Welcome to the third dimension. While AI has been revolutionizing 2D images and video, a new frontier has decisively opened: the ability to generate 3D models and environments from text, images, or a combination of inputs.

This is the art of sculpting in the void—of speaking form into existence. This development is poised to revolutionize industries from gaming and architecture to product design and education, with projections suggesting AI-generated models could match human-crafted quality for up to 60% of basic applications within the next five years. This chapter will serve as your guide to this new world, exploring the fundamental concepts, the essential tools in the digital sculptor's toolkit, and the unique art of prompting for form and space.

The Third Dimension of AI: Core Concepts

Understanding the fundamental technologies behind AI 3D generation is key to harnessing its power. These are the new chisels and clays of our digital workshop.

Text-to-3D: Speaking Sculptures into Existence. This is the most direct and magical form of 3D creation. Sophisticated neural networks interpret your textual descriptions to create detailed 3D models from scratch. It is the ultimate democratization of 3D modeling, allowing anyone to generate a complex object without needing to master intricate software like Blender or ZBrush. The process involves a text encoder that analyzes the meaning of your prompt and a 3D generator that produces the model based on that analysis, all trained on vast datasets of paired text and 3D model examples.

Image-to-3D: Giving Photographs Depth and Form. This technique is like being a digital alchemist, turning flat, 2D images into solid, three-dimensional objects. It uses deep learning algorithms to analyze one or more images and infer a 3D structure. The AI learns patterns, shadows, and perspectives from the images to construct a plausible 3D model. This is particularly revolutionary in architecture, where it can create 3D building models from 2D blueprints, or in entertainment, for generating 3D characters from 2D concept art.

Neural Radiance Fields (NeRFs): Capturing a Scene in a Bottle. NeRF is a cutting-edge technology that creates photorealistic, navigable 3D scenes from a collection of 2D images taken from different viewpoints. Instead of creating a traditional 3D model made of polygons (a mesh), it represents the scene as a continuous volumetric function—a "field" that understands how light radiates through that space. This allows for incredibly realistic renderings of light, reflections, and transparent objects. This technology is being heavily explored by major players like NVIDIA and Google. Even consumer-facing tools like Midjourney are introducing "NeRF-like" 3D capabilities in V7, allowing you to take a generated 2D image and move the camera around the scene to create new images from different angles, effectively letting you walk around inside your creation.

The Digital Sculptor's Toolkit: Tools in Focus

The ecosystem of AI 3D tools is growing rapidly. While many are still in development, several key platforms are leading the charge in 2025.

Womp: An emerging platform that is gaining significant traction for its user-friendly, web-based approach to creating AI-generated 3D models. It is particularly popular for applications in e-commerce and product visualization, allowing brands to quickly generate 3D versions of their products.

NVIDIA's Suite (GANverse3D, AI Playground, Omniverse): As a leader in graphics and AI, NVIDIA is a dominant force in this space. Their suite of tools offers a comprehensive ecosystem for 3D creation. **GANverse3D** specializes in creating realistic 3D models from 2D images, while the web-based **AI Playground** provides an accessible interface for text-to-3D generation. These technologies are integrated into **NVIDIA Omniverse**, a powerful collaborative platform for real-time 3D simulation and design.

Autodesk's Generative Design Tools: A titan of traditional 3D software, Autodesk has deeply integrated

218

AI into its products like Creo and ArchiCAD. These tools feature

Generative Design, where an engineer or architect can input a set of functional requirements and constraints (e.g., "design a chair that can support 300 pounds, uses the least amount of material, and can be 3D printed"), and the AI will automatically generate thousands of optimized 3D design solutions.

Prompting for Form and Space: A Practical Guide

Prompting for 3D generation requires a shift in thinking. You are no longer just describing a flat picture; you are defining an object with volume, texture, and a relationship to the space around it. You must become a sculptor, an architect, and a materials scientist all at once.

Describing Geometry: Use clear, literal language to define the object's shape, size, and structure. Precision is your friend. Instead of "a chair," specify "a Queen Anne style armchair with cabriole legs, a high, curved back, and scrolled arms." Instead of "a sword," describe "a Japanese katana with a curved, single-edged blade, a circular handguard (tsuba), and a hilt wrapped in black silk."

Defining Materials and Textures: This is absolutely crucial for realism. A 3D model is just a shape until you tell the AI what it's made of. Your prompts must include specific material descriptors. Think about how light interacts with the surface.

Instead of "wood," try "`rough-hewn oak wood` with a `matte finish`."

Instead of "plastic," try "`glossy, translucent amber-colored plastic`."

Instead of "metal," try "`tarnished brass` with a `patinated green sheen.`"

Specifying Environment and Lighting: A 3D model's appearance is heavily influenced by how light interacts with its surfaces. Even if you only want the model itself, describing the lighting helps the AI render it correctly.

For neutral presentation: "`Rendered in a white void with soft, diffused studio lighting` from the top-left."

For dramatic effect: "`Rendered with dramatic, high-contrast chiaroscuro lighting` that casts long shadows."

Synthesizing Thinking Styles for 3D: The most effective 3D prompts blend all three thinking styles we've discussed throughout this book. Let's create a truly unique object.

Literal Thinking: "Generate a 3D model of a vintage, overstuffed armchair."

Lateral Thinking: "Design it to look as if it is carved from a single, giant, ripe avocado."

Technical Thinking: "The main body of the chair should have the `matte, slightly bumpy texture of an avocado skin`. The seat cushion should be a perfectly round, `polished wooden sphere` representing the avocado pit. Render the final model with `soft, warm studio lighting` to highlight its organic forms."

By mastering this new form of prompting, you can now design and visualize objects, characters, and entire worlds with unprecedented speed and creative freedom. The void of the digital screen is no longer a flat canvas; it is a block of marble, waiting for your words to give it form.

Crafting Impactful Prompts Across Platforms: A Multi-Tool Approach to Fashion Brand Development

Welcome to the conductor's podium. Throughout this book, we have explored the individual instruments in our digital orchestra—the powerful language models, the visionary image generators, the cinematic video tools, and the symphonic music composers. Now, it is time to bring them all together. This chapter is our grand performance, a practical journey where we will step into the role of the "AI Orchestrator" to build an entire brand from a single idea to a full-fledged advertising campaign.

We will move fluidly between different AI platforms, selecting the right tool for each specific task. We'll use LLMs for strategy, image generators for branding, and a suite of video tools to create a compelling ad film. This is where the theory becomes practice, demonstrating how to craft impactful, tool-specific prompts that work in harmony to achieve a complex creative goal. Let's begin our composition.

1. Brand Inception: From Idea to Identity

Every great brand starts with a spark of an idea. Our idea is a sustainable, high-end fashion brand. Our first task is to give it a name and a face.

Finding the Perfect Brand Name (Using ChatGPT or Claude)

For a creative and strategic task like naming, we turn to a powerful Large Language Model like **ChatGPT (GPT-4o)** or **Anthropic's Claude 4**. Their strength lies in brainstorming, understanding nuance, and generating a wide array of creative options.

Prompt Formula: "Act as an expert [****]. Generate **[Number]** unique name ideas for a [****] brand that focuses on [****]. The brand's target audience is [****] who value **[Core Customer Values]**. For each name, provide a brief rationale for why it works."

Example Prompt: "Act as an expert **Brand Strategist specializing in luxury eco-conscious brands**. Generate **10** unique name ideas for a **sustainable, high-end fashion brand** that focuses on **minimalist designs and ethically-sourced, natural materials**. The brand's target audience is **urban professionals aged 25-40** who value **timeless style, environmental responsibility, and transparent production**. For each name, provide a brief rationale for why it works."

Let's say the AI returns a great option: **"Aura Terra"**. It combines the ethereal feeling of "Aura" with the grounded, earthy "Terra," perfectly capturing our brand's essence.

Designing the Logo (Switching to Midjourney or Imagen 4)

With our name, "Aura Terra," we now need a visual identity. We switch instruments to an image generation tool. For this, **Midjourney V7** is an excellent choice for its aesthetic quality, while **Google's Imagen 4** is a strong contender for its superior ability to render clean text.

Prompt Formula (for Midjourney V7): "[****] logo design for a brand named ['****']. The logo should incorporate elements that suggest [****]. The typography should be [****]. Use a color palette of [****]. The design must be [****], on a [****] --ar 1:1 --style raw"

Example Prompt (for Midjourney V7): "**Minimalist vector logo** design for a sustainable fashion brand named '**Aura Terra**'. The logo should subtly incorporate a **stylized leaf motif within the letter 'A' of Aura**. The typography for 'Aura Terra' should be an **elegant, modern sans-serif font, clean and legible**. Use a color palette of **muted earth tones, specifically olive green and warm beige**. The design must be **simple, sophisticated, and scalable for use on clothing tags and large storefront signs**, on a **plain white background** --ar 1:1 --style raw"

2. Brand Strategy Development (Back to ChatGPT or Claude)

225

A brand is more than a name and a logo; it needs a soul and a plan. We return to our LLM, which excels at strategic thinking and long-form text generation, to build the brand's core strategy.

Prompt Formula: "Act as a [****]. Develop a comprehensive brand strategy for [****], a [****] brand.

Brand Essence: [****] **Target Audience:** [****]

Please structure the strategy with these specific sections:

Brand Positioning Statement: A concise summary of our unique place in the market.

Three Key Brand Pillars: The core principles that guide our brand.

Target Audience Persona: A detailed profile of our ideal customer, "Alex."

Competitor Analysis: Identify and analyze 3 main competitors.

Unique Selling Proposition (USP): What makes us different and better.

Brand Voice and Tone Guidelines: How our brand should communicate.

Key Marketing Channels: Where we will reach our audience."

Example Prompt: "Act as a **Senior Brand Strategist from a top-tier marketing agency**. Develop a comprehensive brand strategy for **Aura Terra**, a **sustainable high-end fashion brand**.

Brand Essence: Minimalist design, ethically-sourced materials, transparency, and timeless style. Target Audience: Urban professionals aged 25-40.

Please structure the strategy with these specific sections:

Brand Positioning Statement

Three Key Brand Pillars

Target Audience Persona

Competitor Analysis

Unique Selling Proposition (USP)

Brand Voice and Tone Guidelines

Key Marketing Channels"

3. Creating Social Media Content (A Multimodal Symphony)

Now we execute the strategy. This requires a fluid workflow, switching between text and visual generation tools.

3.1 The Content Calendar (ChatGPT or Claude)

First, we need a plan. An LLM is perfect for organizing ideas into a structured calendar.

Example Prompt: "Create a one-week social media content calendar for Aura Terra for Instagram. The content should be a mix of formats (Reel, Carousel Post, Story). For each day, provide the format, a post idea, a sample caption, and 5 relevant hashtags, all aligned with the brand's sophisticated and conscious tone."

3.2 Visual Content Creation (Midjourney V7)

Next, we create the visuals for our posts. We use Midjourney V7 to ensure a consistent, high-end aesthetic.

Example Prompt (for a Carousel Post): "Photorealistic lifestyle image for a sustainable fashion brand. A woman with a confident, serene expression wears a minimalist beige linen dress. She is standing in a sun-drenched, airy loft with large windows and lush green plants in the background. The lighting is soft and natural. The overall mood is calm, sophisticated, and elegant. --ar 4:5 --style raw"

3.3 Video Content Creation (Midjourney + Runway)

For a modern brand, video is non-negotiable. We'll create a short, 10-second promotional Reel. This is a two-step process.

Step 1: Generate a Key Image in Midjourney Prompt: "*A stunning close-up shot of a woman's face, her eyes closed as if enjoying a gentle breeze. Her skin has a natural, healthy glow. Soft, golden hour lighting. The mood is peaceful and serene. --ar 9:16 --style raw*"

Step 2: Animate the Image in Runway Gen-4 We take the generated image and upload it to **Runway**. Then, we use a simple prompt to add subtle motion. **Prompt:** *"The woman's hair gently blows in the wind. A subtle, slow zoom-in on her face."*

3.4 Post Copy (Back to ChatGPT or Claude)

Finally, we return to our LLM to write the compelling captions for our visuals.

Example Prompt (for the Reel): *"Write an engaging Instagram Reel caption for Aura Terra. The video shows a woman's face in serene close-up. The caption should evoke a feeling of peace and connection with nature. It should subtly hint at the sustainable materials of our clothing without being overly technical. End with a gentle call-to-action and 5 relevant hashtags."*

Mastering AI-Assisted Ad Film Creation: A Comprehensive Guide

Now for our masterpiece: a full 60-second ad film. This is the ultimate test of the AI Orchestrator, requiring a seamless blend of multiple tools and techniques.

The AI-Assisted Ad Film Creation Process

1. The Brief: Laying the Foundation Every great film starts with a clear brief. We'll use an LLM to expand a simple idea into a detailed concept.

Prompt Formula for Brief Expansion: "Expand the following one-line brief into a detailed advertising concept: Brief: [Insert one-line brief]. Please provide: 1. Target audience description, 2. Key message to convey, 3. Desired emotional response, 4. Unique selling proposition, 5. Call to action, 6. Brand tone and style guidelines."

2. Ideation and Concept Development With the brief defined, we use the LLM to brainstorm creative concepts for the film.

Prompt Formula for Concept Ideation: "Based on the following brief details, generate 3 unique concept ideas for an ad film: Target Audience: [Insert target audience], Key Message: [Insert key message].

For each concept, provide: 1. A catchy title, 2. A one-sentence synopsis, 3. A key visual element, 4. A potential tagline."

3. Script Creation Once a concept is chosen (e.g., "Threads of Change"), we have the LLM write a full script.

Prompt Formula for Script Writing: "Write a script for a `[duration]` ad film based on the concept: Title: `[Insert concept title]`. The script should include: 1. Scene descriptions, 2. Dialogue or Voice-over text, 3. On-screen text, 4. Music and sound effect notes. Format it in standard screenplay format."

4. Storyboarding and Shot Division We then have the AI break the script into a shot list, creating our production blueprint.

Prompt Formula for Shot Division: "Divide the following script into individual shots for storyboarding. For each shot, provide: 1. Shot number, 2. Shot type (e.g., wide, medium, close-up), 3. Brief description of the action, 4. Dialogue/VO, 5. Duration (in seconds). Script: `[Insert full script here]`."

5. Theme and Style Selection This step is about defining the film's look and feel. We can use an LLM to suggest visual styles.

6. Prompt Creation for Visuals (The Director's Vision) Now, we translate each shot from our storyboard into a detailed image prompt for a tool like **Midjourney V7**.

231

Prompt Formula for Image Generation: "Create a Midjourney prompt for Shot #[Number]: `of`. The visual style is `` ` ``. The prompt should include subject, setting, lighting, color palette, and camera angle. Format as: `[Full prompt] --ar 16:9`."

7. Animation and Video Generation (The Final Cut) This is where we bring the still images to life. For 2025, this is a multi-tool process.

For shots without dialogue, we can use **Image-to-Video** in **Runway Gen-4** or **Luma Dream Machine**.

For shots with complex motion, we can use **Text-to-Video** in a tool like **Kling**.

For shots with dialogue, we must use a tool with **lip-sync** capabilities, like **Google's Veo 3** or **Kling**.

Example Prompt (for a Text-to-Video shot in Kling): "*A woman walks through a bustling city market, smiling. She is wearing a flowing white dress from Aura Terra. The scene is vibrant and full of life. [Motion Instructions] The camera does a smooth tracking shot, following her from the side. Cinematic style, warm natural lighting.*"

8. Sound and Music Finally, we add the audio layer. We can use a tool like **SUNO** to generate a custom musical score based on a prompt describing the film's mood ("*uplifting, gentle, orchestral score with piano and strings*") and use another tool to generate sound effects.

Case Study: "Teri Yaad" - Crafting a Music Video with AI Avatars

Let's move from a hypothetical ad film to a real-world creative project: the music video for my song "Teri Yaad." This project showcases a complete, modern AI workflow, combining custom music generation, advanced character creation, and multi-tool video production to bring a creative vision to life.

1. The Brief & The Creative Spark: The core concept was to create a music video for "Teri Yaad" (meaning "Your Memory"), a song about love and longing. Instead of using human actors, the vision was to feature two AI-generated avatars, "Rumi" and "Ira," to tell the story. The creative process began not with a prompt, but with a human feeling—I hummed a simple melody, a "dhun," into my phone's voice recorder. This raw, human-centric idea became the seed for the entire project.

2. The AI-Orchestrated Workflow:

Music Generation (SUNO): The first step was to transform my recorded hum into a full song. I used **SUNO's Audio Upload** feature, providing my acapella recording as the initial input. I then prompted SUNO with the style: *"A soulful, melancholic Indian pop song with acoustic guitar, gentle tabla beats, and a string section."* SUNO analyzed the melody from my recording and built the entire instrumental arrangement around it, creating the final track for "Teri Yaad."

Character Creation (Flux + LoRA): To create our AI singers, Rumi and Ira, I first used the image generator **Flux** to design their base appearance. Once I had a definitive look for each, I used a set of 15-20 images of each character to train a custom **LoRA (Low-Rank Adaptation) model**. This advanced technique creates a small, specialized AI model for each character, which can then be used with a base model to generate new images of that specific character with incredible consistency.

Storyboarding with Prompts (Flux + LoRA): With the LoRA models for Rumi and Ira ready, I created the visual storyboard. Each shot was a detailed prompt in Flux, now including the special trigger word for the character's LoRA.

Example Prompt: *"A photorealistic image of **Rumi-Lora**, a young man with sad eyes, looking out a rain-streaked window at a neon-lit city street at night. Melancholic mood, cinematic lighting, shallow depth of field."*

Animation & Lip-Sync (Kling): The generated storyboard images were then brought to life using **Kling**, a powerful video generation tool known for its motion quality and lip-sync capabilities. For each shot, I used an **Image-to-Video** prompt.

Example Prompt: *"Animate this image. Rumi-Lora slowly turns his head towards the camera, a single tear* *rolling down his cheek. The rain on the window streaks downwards."* For the singing shots, Kling's lip-sync feature was crucial, animating the characters' mouths to match the vocals from the SUNO-generated track.

3. The Final Render: The animated clips from Kling were compiled in a video editor, synchronized with the "Teri Yaad" audio track, and color-graded to create the final, cohesive music video.

Key Takeaways from This Modern Workflow:

The Power of the Human Seed: The entire project, for all its technical complexity, grew from a simple, human-generated melody. This highlights that AI is at its most powerful when it serves to amplify a core human idea.

Advanced Consistency is Here: The use of custom-trained LoRA models demonstrates that creating consistent, recognizable AI characters for narrative projects is no longer a dream but a practical reality.

The AI Orchestrator is Essential: This project was a symphony of specialized tools. Success depended on knowing which instrument to use for each part of the composition: SUNO for audio, Flux for visuals, and Kling for animation.

New Creative Frontiers: The ability to create and direct AI avatars opens up entirely new avenues for storytelling, allowing creators to produce compelling narratives without the constraints of physical production. This case study illustrates a complete, end-to-end creative process that is uniquely possible in 2025, blending human emotion with a powerful and diverse orchestra of AI tools.

The Human Touch: When Not to Use AI

As we conclude our journey through the landscape of AI-assisted creativity, it's crucial to step back and consider the bigger picture. While AI tools have revolutionized many aspects of creative work, they are not a panacea. In this final chapter, we'll explore the importance of maintaining a human touch in our creative endeavors, discussing the risks of over-reliance on AI, the value of preserving human skills, and how to strike the right balance between human creativity and AI assistance.

The Risk of AI Dependency

In our enthusiasm for the capabilities of AI, it's easy to fall into the trap of over-reliance. Like a gardener becoming too dependent on power tools and forgetting the nuanced touch needed to nurture delicate plants, creatives risk losing their innate skills and intuitions by leaning too heavily on AI.

One of the primary risks of AI dependency is the potential for homogenization of creative output. When many creators use the same AI tools with similar prompts, there's a danger of producing work that lacks distinctive character. Just as a forest thrives on biodiversity, the creative world needs a variety of unique voices and perspectives to remain vibrant and innovative.

Moreover, over-reliance on AI can lead to a diminished ability to think critically and solve problems independently. Creative work often involves navigating ambiguity, making intuitive leaps, and drawing from personal experiences – areas where AI, despite its capabilities, cannot fully replace human cognition.

There's also the risk of becoming detached from the creative process itself. The joy of creation, the struggle with ideas, and the satisfaction of overcoming creative challenges are integral parts of the artistic journey. Outsourcing too much of this process to AI can lead to a sense of disconnection from one's work.

Furthermore, excessive dependence on AI can stifle the development of new skills and techniques. If we always turn to AI for solutions, we may miss opportunities to grow and evolve as creatives. It's through grappling with challenges that we often make our most significant breakthroughs and discoveries.

Lastly, there's the ethical consideration of authenticity and originality. As AI-generated content becomes more prevalent, there's a growing concern about the blurring lines between human and machine-created work. This raises questions about authorship, creativity, and the value we place on human-generated ideas.

To mitigate these risks, it's essential to approach AI as a tool in our creative toolkit, not as a replacement for our own creative faculties. Use AI to enhance your work, but don't let it define or limit your creative expression. Remember, the most compelling creative works often come from a place of personal experience, emotion, and unique perspective – elements that AI cannot replicate.

Preserving and Developing Human Skills

In the age of AI, preserving and developing distinctly human skills is not just beneficial – it's essential. These skills are what set us apart and allow us to use AI tools effectively while maintaining our unique creative voice.

Critical thinking and problem-solving are paramount. While AI can process vast amounts of data and generate solutions, it lacks the nuanced understanding of context and the ability to make judgment calls based on complex, often intangible factors. Cultivate your ability to analyze situations, question assumptions, and approach problems from multiple angles.

Emotional intelligence is another crucial human skill. The ability to understand and convey complex emotions, to empathize with an audience, and to create work that resonates on a deep, personal level is uniquely human. This emotional depth is what often separates good creative work from truly impactful art.

Curiosity and continuous learning are vital in a rapidly changing world. Instead of relying on AI to provide all the answers, nurture your sense of wonder. Explore new ideas, techniques, and perspectives. The broader and deeper your knowledge base, the more creative and original your work will be, even when assisted by AI.

Develop your intuition and trust your instincts. While AI operates on algorithms and data, human intuition draws from a lifetime of experiences and subconscious pattern recognition. This gut feeling often leads to innovative ideas and solutions that AI might not generate.

Hone your craft manually. Whether it's sketching, writing longhand, or practicing an instrument, engaging in the physical aspects of your craft helps maintain a connection to the creative process. These tactile experiences often spark ideas and solutions that might not emerge when working solely with digital tools.

Collaboration and communication skills remain critically important. The ability to work effectively with others, to articulate ideas clearly, and to give and receive constructive feedback are skills that AI cannot replace. These interpersonal abilities often lead to the cross-pollination of ideas and the creation of truly innovative work.

Finally, cultivate mindfulness and self-awareness. Understanding your own creative process, recognizing your strengths and weaknesses, and being aware of how you respond to different creative challenges are crucial for personal growth and for using AI tools effectively.

By consciously preserving and developing these human skills, you ensure that AI remains a tool that enhances your creativity rather than a crutch that limits it. Your unique combination of skills, experiences, and perspectives is what will allow you to use AI in ways that are truly innovative and personal.

Finding the Right Balance: Human Creativity and AI Assistance

Striking the right balance between human creativity and AI assistance is akin to conducting an orchestra – it requires finesse, intuition, and a deep understanding of the strengths of each component. The goal is to create a harmonious blend where AI amplifies human creativity without overshadowing it.

Start by clearly defining your creative vision. Before turning to AI, spend time developing your ideas, sketching out concepts, and identifying the core message or emotion you want to convey. This human-generated foundation will guide your use of AI tools, ensuring they serve your vision rather than dictate it.

Use AI for inspiration, not imitation. When facing creative blocks, AI can be a valuable brainstorming partner. However, treat AI-generated ideas as starting points, not final products. Use them to spark your own creativity, then build upon and transform these ideas with your unique perspective and skills.

Leverage AI for technical tasks and iterations. AI excels at repetitive tasks, technical optimizations, and generating variations. Use it to handle time-consuming aspects of your work, freeing you to focus on the big-picture creative decisions that require human judgment and intuition.

Maintain a critical eye. Always evaluate AI-generated content through the lens of your expertise and artistic sensibility. Don't hesitate to modify, combine, or completely discard AI suggestions if they don't align with your vision. Remember, you are the creator, and AI is your tool.

Embrace the iterative process. Use AI as part of an iterative creative cycle. Generate ideas or content with AI, then refine and expand upon them with your human touch. Return to AI for further iterations or technical assistance as needed. This back-and-forth process can lead to results that are both innovative and personally meaningful.

Recognize AI's limitations. Understand that while AI is powerful, it has blind spots. It may lack cultural nuance, struggle with highly abstract concepts, or fail to capture subtle emotional tones. In these areas, human insight is irreplaceable. Know when to step in and provide the context, emotion, or nuance that AI might miss.

Preserve the human element in your work. Ensure that your personal experiences, emotions, and unique perspective shine through in your final product. These elements are what make your work distinctly yours and create a connection with your audience.

Continuously educate yourself. Stay informed about AI capabilities and limitations. The more you understand these tools, the better you can integrate them into your creative process without becoming overly reliant on them.

Reflect on your process. Regularly step back and assess how you're using AI in your work. Are you using it to enhance your creativity or as a shortcut? Are you still challenging yourself and growing as a creator? Adjust your approach as needed to maintain a healthy balance.

Remember, the most powerful creative works often emerge from the synergy between human imagination and technological capabilities. By finding the right balance, you can harness the strengths of AI while preserving the uniquely human elements that make your work meaningful and impactful.

As we navigate this new era of AI-assisted creativity, let us remember that our most valuable asset is our humanity. Our experiences, emotions, intuitions, and unique perspectives are what breathe life into our creations. AI is a powerful tool, but it is just that – a tool. The magic happens when human creativity dances with artificial intelligence, each enhancing the other, creating something greater than the sum of its parts. As you move forward in your creative journey, carry with you the knowledge and skills you've gained, but never lose sight of the human touch that makes your work truly yours.

www.ingramcontent.com/pod-product-compliance
Lightning Source LLC
LaVergne TN
LVHW051226050326
832903LV00028B/2263

Prompt DOT AI: Mastering the Art of Creativity in the Age of
AI" takes readers on an insightful voyage through the
fascinating world of AI prompting.

This book unravels the magic behind crafting powerful
prompts that drive AI to produce captivating outputs. With a
mix of real-life examples, practical guidelines, and
thought-provoking insights,

Da Sachin makes the art of AI prompting an exciting and
attainable skill. This book serves as a valuable guide for
anyone, from AI beginners to experienced practitioners,
offering fresh perspectives on the boundless potentials of
AI-enabled creativity.

www.xdotai.in
www.dasachin.com
@xdotai.in

ISBN 9798854960342

90000

9 798854 960342